KINGDOM ENCOUNTER
DISCIPLESHIP

Michael & Michele Kole

Unless otherwise noted, Scripture quotations are taken from the NEW SPIRIT-FILLED LIFE BIBLE, New
King James Version, Executive Editor Jack W Hayford, 2002 by Thomas Nelson, Inc.

ISBN: 979-8-218-25207-6
Independently Published

DEDICATION

The KINGDOM ENCOUNTER DISCIPLESHIP is lovingly dedicated to our Heavenly Father, to Jesus Christ our Lord and Savior, and the Holy Spirit. To YOU belong all praise, glory, and honor!

ACKNOWLEDGEMENTS

SPECIAL ACKNOWLEDGEMENTS
Our Pastors – 2012 to Present:

Jurgen & Leanne Matthesius (Awaken Church San Diego - Founders and Lead Pastors),
Jon & Becky Heinrichs (Awaken Church Central Region Pastors)
Thank you for your support and encouragement. Opening doors of opportunity, trusting
us to prove ourselves through faith in our Lord Jesus Christ and by the power of His
Holy Spirit, to find the gold within and encouragement to keep digging!
We honor and love you! It is a privilege to serve in this ministry!

ACKNOWLEDGEMENTS
Our Pastors from September 29, 1986, to 2012

John Maxwell (Sr. Pastor Skyline Wesleyan Church), Mike MacIntosh (Sr. Pastor Horizon
Christian Fellowship), George Runyan (Pastor & Apostolic leader in San Diego), Cesar &
Claudia Castellanos (Founder of the G12, Bogota, Columbia)

SPECIAL THANKS TO THE COUPLE
Who Discipled Us and Inspired Our Future

Bill & Marianne Klaussen
(Skyline Wesleyan Church, Navigators Discipleship Program – 1986)

CONTENTS

KINGDOM ENCOUNTER DISCIPLESHIP

Training Disciples to Disciple Others

Jesus Christ, as He left this earth to be with His Heavenly Father, told His disciples along with all those present for His ascension: "[19] Therefore, go and make disciples of all the nations, baptizing them in the name of the Father and the Son and the Holy Spirit. [20] Teach these new disciples to obey all the commands I have given you. And be sure of this: I am with you always, even to the end of the age." Matthew 28:19-20 (NLT)

The KINGDOM ENCOUNTER DISCIPLESHIP is designed to assist believers to grow in their faith, maturing in their identity as a son or daughter of GOD ALMIGHTY, and learning how to live a KINGDOM LIFESTYLE in this present age. They become aware that God has a specific destiny and purpose for their life, which includes becoming a disciple and making disciples in addition to their calling as a King and Priest in the marketplace, their family and ministry.

We believe that we are individual members of the Body of Christ with a unique assignment on our life: *"For we are His workmanship, created in Christ Jesus for good works, which God prepared beforehand that we should walk in them. Ephesians 2:10 (NKJV)*. His Holy Spirit empowers believers to fulfill their individual calling and the greater commandment to Disciple Nations.

This discipleship manual/workbook has been prepared for the benefit of the individual together with a small group of 2-3 fellow disciples. *The value of the KINGDOM ENCOUNTER DISCIPLESHIP is found in completing the sessions one at a time, then discussing each one before moving on to the next. The small group together gains clarity, wisdom, knowledge, and practical application as they learn from the session and their fellow disciples.*

THE WHY AND HOW OF SMALL GROUP DISCIPLESHIP:

Over 30 years discipling in small groups, working with home groups and developing leaders has taught us valuable lessons about effective discipleship. As Jesus chose twelve men, then 3 (James, Peter, and John) for special teaching, we have found that a small group of three, all men or all women, works as the best model to effectively learn and grow as a disciple. Although four people is workable, beyond that someone is always left out of the discussion. Due to the differences in the way men and women like to discuss or share points, keeping the groups homogenous encourages everyone to participate, fewer ego issues, and more transparency.

The KINGDOM ENCOUNTER DISCIPLESHIP was first given to two groups, approximately fifteen men and 15 women from January – July 2023, at Awaken Church, San Diego, where we are all members. We met to discuss each individual session every other Saturday from 7 – 9 am. Each group was divided into small groups of 3-4 each, while meeting in a large room with clusters of tables and chairs. The sessions were given in order and disciples were given 2 weeks to complete the material. Between the groups, were

Training Disciples to Disciple Others
Continued…

several couples who said they worked together to complete the lessons; and some groups checked with each other as they completed the lessons or had questions.

The small groups were instructed to appoint a different person for each session to facilitate the group, which keeps it moving along so that the whole session could be discussed within two hours. The purpose is to train confident disciples to know how to disciple others. The small groups stayed connected during the week, prayed for each other, and kept each other accountable to finish their session. ***The value of this form of discipleship is in the discussion***, so each one learns from the others. Disciples learned that there may not be any one correct answer but how the Holy Spirit speaks and reveals his Rhema Word individually to them throughout the sessions.

When the small groups meet in a large church setting, the leaders are encouraged to give completion certificates at the end of KINGDOM ENCOUNTER DISCIPLESHIP. Once individuals have completed the sessions, we encourage each of them to invite others to start a new series. The KINGDOM ENCOUNTER DISCIPLESHIP may be conducted in a variety of settings: in a large group – with individual groups of 3-4, or around the kitchen table at home, a coffee shop or in other appropriate settings.

The KINGDOM ENCOUNTER DISCIPLESHIP is designed to be effective for training disciples to disciple others. Successful discipleship requires love for one another, prayer, commitment, consistency, and accountability, by the Word of God, as taught by Jesus Christ, in the Power of the Holy Spirit.

TO HIM BE ALL GLORY AND HONOR, In Jesus Name. Amen.

It is our heart's desire to see God's people secure in their identity as His children, experiencing the Kingdom of God in this life, and fully empowered to make disciples of all nations.

For further information or questions about how to implement a KINGDOM ENCOUNTER DISCIPLESHIP at your church, please text/call either Michael Kole at 858-848-4274 or Michele Kole at 858-344-5998. Email: michaelkole1@gmail.com, michelekole@gmail.com

How to set up successful KINGDOM ENCOUNTER Discussion Groups

The most value from **Kingdom Encounter Discipleship** will be realized when individuals complete their sessions then meet in small groups (3-4 max) to discuss what the Holy Spirit has revealed to them. Due to the length of the lessons, generally 2 weeks will be necessary to complete each session. **We recommend doing the sessions in order, one at a time, then followed by the discussion in the small group**. We have learned that the value is in the discussion – *"As iron sharpens iron, so a man sharpens the countenance of his friend." Proverbs 27:17*

Setting up the Discussion Groups: Whether there are several groups meeting in a large space or in smaller settings, individuals should separate themselves into groups of 3-4 each, preferably homogenous. We have found that groups larger than 4 tend to be less successful because the discussion gets bogged down, and people tend to hide out and rely on others to do the work for them. As mentioned previously, we have discovered over years of discipling that men and women like to discuss things differently and especially between spouses. There is more transparency, fewer ego issues and less personality dominance when the groups are homogeneous. If spouses like to write out their lessons together that of course Is fine. **Discipleship is about growing and maturing in one's own identity as a child of God.**

WHEN IT'S YOUR TURN TO BE THE DISCUSSION LEADER – In the small group, choose a discussion leader on a rotating basis for each session. That individual is **not teaching the lesson**, rather **facilitating the discussion**. Here's how to do it:
1. The Leader for the session opens in prayer to bless the time together.
2. Then begins the discussion around the 1st section of the Lesson.
3. You may take up to 10 minutes to highlight praise reports/make requests or record answered prayer before moving into the lesson. A prayer sheet with a list of your members is at the beginning of each session.
4. At the end of the lesson, **choose a new leader** for the following session. Each person in the group will have the opportunity to lead several times.
5. The purpose of small group discipleship is to raise up confident leaders to be able to disciple others.

THE DISCUSSION TIME:
Start with the first section in the lesson. Many find going point by point works fine; and asking each person to give their thoughts on a particular point. Or you can use the questions below to stimulate the discussion.

1. What did the Holy Spirit reveal to you in this section? (A Rhema word?)
2. Are there any questions or comments about anything in this section?
3. What did you learn that seems different than what you thought you knew before?

How to set up successful KINGDOM ENCOUNTER Discussion Groups
Continued…

4. What did you have for the summary of the verses in the section?

NOTE: If there is no immediate response, you give your answer to one of the points in the lesson and ask the others what they wrote.

Move on to the next section – be mindful of the time frame so that you can get to all the sections rather than get bogged down in just one area. Each person may have a section they really want covered toward the end of the lesson.

The leader of the session oversees moving the discussion along so everyone gets to participate. If someone is dominating a discussion, thank them for their thoughts, but ask for someone else's ideas around the topic. Do not be afraid to say, "Let's move on" or "Let's come back to this one at the end if we have time."

When there are multiple small groups meeting, the Discipleship Leader may get the groups together at the end to hear from each small group. The small group leader can summarize what the overall takeaways from their discussions were or designate another person in their group to do so.

PLEASE BE MINDFUL – we love each other and are concerned about what's going on in each other's lives. However, this is a time set aside to receive from the **KINGDOM ENCOUNTER** lesson at hand. If there is ministry or prayer time needed agree to set time at the end of the lesson, or away from the small group meeting. **This is not a time to catch up on each other's weekly activities – save that for before or after.**

TESTIMONIALS

What people are saying about KINGDOM ENCOUNTER DISCIPLESHIP:

In Matthew 28:19, Jesus gives a mandate to "Go and Make Disciples". Many churches have focused on "making believers". Kingdom Encounter gives each church a curriculum to take the believer into what it means to be a disciple. If you or your small group are hungry to grow in the knowledge of what discipleship looks like, then Kingdom Encounter is for you. It is not only foundational but also challenging in its approach. I fully endorse this study for believers that want to go the next step...Discipleship.

Ken Gargula / Awaken Church Connect Group Leader

"Every lesson brings me closer to Him. I believe this course is a must for both new and old believers. Michael and Michele have been anointed with a beautiful ability to lead – I am incredibly grateful to them for creating this class. I highly recommend Kingdom Encounter to every believer. Etirsa I.

I particularly enjoy being able to discuss the material with fellow students and share all that God has been revealing to each of us along this journey! I have thoroughly enjoyed observing how my husband has grown in his faith as a result of being immersed in this program. Gail W.

The biggest take away for me from Kingdom Encounter was in the revelation of the KINGDOM OF GOD itself. In all of my years as a Christian, I have somehow missed the fact that the Kingdom of God is here and that the Kingdom of God is inside of me!!! This was the most eye-opening revelation for me. Michelle H.

This is the first time I am involved in a discipleship, and I am so excited for how God will use me to teach others. This program helped me to understand my true identity in Christ, how we are Kings and Priests here on earth and our mission is to live in this principle. The application of these sessions in my life has helped me to minister, pray and trust God in such a different way. My faith is stronger, and I have a deeper relationship with God. Samuel I.

Kingdom Encounter is a thoughtfully organized study, and one I highly recommend for anyone who wants to learn the foundations of faith in the one true God and be equipped to disciple others!
Susan B

The workbook was well put together and is such a great tool to have and use to help believers of all levels of maturity to grow and to share their faith. Sylvia T.

TESTIMONIALS
Continued

My favorite class was the first one I took which was "The Kingdom – Present and Future". It reminded me of how blessed I am to be part of the Kingdom as well as reminded me of everything that our Lord has blessed us with that we should never take for granted. Marta C.

I have a broader view of the kingdom operating on earth through the Holy Spirit and His believers. Pat M.

The Kingdom Encounter is an amazing course on how to disciple. How to increase Christlikeness in character and behavior in my life. Learning ways to improve my prayer life and my walk with God. Sandy B.

He shakes the chaff off the wheat that accumulated in my spiritual walk over these past 47 years and in His perfect provision, brought the Kingdom Encounter into my life at this most opportune moment. I'm blown away each session with how hungry my spirit is for this well organized and presented approach to the Christian fundamentals I have needed. And the small group discussion that embeds what I've studied in each module is encouraging! My walk feels fresh, new, and as revitalized as it was when it began so many years ago. I feel strong and empowered like never before! Shanti d.

Michael and Michele Kole are great ambassadors of Jesus Christ. The Kingdom Encounter discipleship aligns with the kingdom of God. Through this course the Holy Spirit reveals the depth of our identity, power, authority, obedience when we surrender. The Kingdom Encounter has been part of my identity transformation.   Gabriel C.

We have been so blessed since signing up for Kingdom Encounter from the first session it has challenged us to dig deeper into the subject matter as we rely on the prompting of the Holy Spirit. This is a great tool for encouraging us to prepare to disciple others in the Kingdom. Our confidence has risen as we have studied the various topics relating to discipleship and sharing the gospel. Ted and Joyce H.

I thank God for all He is doing through this teaching to raise up an on fire generation of healthy individuals who are learning how to bring heaven to earth everywhere we go! Thank you both for your obedience and walking it out as an example for all to see. This teaching has changed my life, I honor and appreciate you beyond words! Lisa Ann P.

This is in excellent discipleship program, based upon the Kingdom of God. Even though I have gone through discipleship programs before, and have discipled many others, I still received a lot of benefit in taking this course. Ron D.

KINGDOM ENCOUNTER

IDENTITY
SESSION #1

The KINGDOM OF GOD is available to every believer by faith in the Son of God, and by the power of His Holy Spirit. Knowing and embracing who God created you to be is central to living in HIS Kingdom now.

In this session your "true identity" will unfold; you will learn that you have a unique place in God's design on earth and in His Kingdom. His plan for you originated before the beginning of time. There has never been nor will there ever be anyone like you.

As you start the KINGDOM ENCOUNTER, SESSION #1 – IDENTITY:

This is the foundation for all other sessions, each one builds on the next. First read the **FATHER'S LOVE LETTER**, you will get a glimpse of how special you are to GOD.

Next read the **PARABLE OF THE WING WALKER**, this is all about discovering identity and purpose. This story makes for a great discussion.

Lastly, do the workbook pages on **IDENTITY** and when finished, discuss each section with your small group.

THE FATHER'S
LOVE LETTER

My Child,

You may not know me, but I know everything about you. Psalm 139:1   I know when you sit down and when you rise up. Psalm 139:2   I am familiar with all your ways. Psalm 139:3 Even the very hairs on your head are numbered. Matthew 10:29-31 For you were made in my image. Genesis 1:27 In me you live and move and have your being. Acts 17:28 For you are my offspring. Acts 17:28 I knew you even before you were conceived. Jeremiah 1:4-5   I chose you when I planned creation. Ephesians 1:11-12 You were not a mistake, for all your days are written in my book. Psalm 139:15-16 I determined the exact time of your birth and where you would live. Acts 17:26 You are fearfully and wonderfully made. Psalm 139:14   I knit you together in your mother's womb. Psalm 139:13   And brought you forth on the day you were born. Psalm 71:6 I have been misrepresented by those who don't know me. John 8:41-44 I am not distant and angry, but am the complete expression of love. 1 John 4:16   And it is my desire to lavish my love on you. Simply because you are my child and I am your Father. 1 John 3:1 I offer you more than your earthly father ever could. Matthew 7:11 For I am the perfect father. Matthew 5:48 Every good gift that you receive comes from my hand. James 1:17   For I am your provider and I meet all your needs. Matthew 6:31-33 My plan for your future has always been filled with hope. Jeremiah 29:11   Because I love you with an everlasting love. Jeremiah 31:3   My thoughts toward you are countless as the sand on the seashore. Psalms 139:17-18   And I rejoice over you with singing. Zephaniah 3:17 I will never stop doing good to you. Jeremiah 32:40   For you are my treasured possession. Exodus 19:5   I desire to establish you with all my heart and all my soul Jeremiah 32:41 And I want to show you great and marvelous hings. Jeremiah 33:3   If you seek me with all your heart, you will find me. Deuteronomy 4:29   Delight in me and I will give you the desires of your heart. Psalm 37:4   For it is I who gave you those desires. Philippians 2:13   I am able to do more for you than you could possibly imagine. Ephesians 3:20   For I am your greatest encourager 2 Thessalonians 2:16-17 I am also the Father who comforts you in all your troubles. 2 Corinthians 1:3-4 When you are brokenhearted, I am close to you. Psalm 34:18 As a shepherd carries a lamb, I have carried you close to my heart. Isaiah 40:11   One day I will wipe away every tear from your eyes. Revelation 21:3-4   And I'll take away all the pain you have suffered on this earth. Revelation 21:3-4 I am your Father, and I love you even as I love my son, Jesus. John 17:23 For in Jesus, my love for you is revealed. John 17:26   He is the exact representation of my being. Hebrews 1:3   He came to demonstrate that I am for you, not against you. Romans 8:31   And to tell you that I am not counting your sins. 2 Corinthians 5:18-19 Jesus died so that you and I could be reconciled. 2 Corinthians 5:18-19 His death was the ultimate expression of my love for you. 1 John 4:10   I gave up everything I loved that I might gain your love. Romans 8:31-32   If you receive the gift of my son Jesus, you receive me. 1 John 2:23   And nothing will ever separate you from my love again. Romans 8:38-39   Come home and I'll throw the biggest party heaven has ever seen. Luke 15:7 I have always been Father, and will always be Father. Ephesians 3:14-15 My question is... Will you be my child? John 1:12-13   I am waiting for you. Luke 15:11-32

Love, Your Dad
Almighty God

The **Father's Love Letter** is used by permission, Father Heart Communications © 1999 www.FathersLoveLetter.com

THE PARABLE OF
THE WING WALKER

THE PARABLE OF THE WING WALKER
By Michele Kole

At the end of the GREAT WAR, young men, flush with adrenaline after fighting the enemy from the skies over Europe returned to America. Some of these airmen that flew small biplanes, out of necessity had learned to fix mechanical issues while in flight. They would leave the cockpit, climb out on the wings, and fix the problem; and quickly crawl back into their seat. Dangerous yet exhilarating! And as they say in wartime, *"there are no atheists in foxholes"* and that went especially for these airborne fighters in small biplanes. After living on the edge, returning to the farm or small shop in rural America held no appeal for these flyers. Biplanes left from the war were easy to come by and cheap. The Airshow Circus with Wing Walkers became the rage in this era.

One such airshow circus featured an amazing young Wing Walker, Joe, and his wife, Mary. With a passion for flying and a daredevil at heart, he would fly his plane, named PEARLY GATES, in loop the loops, then steady it, leave the cockpit, crawl out on the wings, and stand proudly waving an American flag, and then swiftly return to the cock pit. His wife, a former gymnast with a heart for danger, was a good match. While he flew, she would do a handstand on the wings to wow the crowd - together they were the star attraction. One spectacular death-defying stunt was with Joe flying the plane upside down with her strapped standing on the wing! Jaw-dropping unbelievable! The rest of the circus performers always said, if these two have a son, he will probably be "Superman"!

In the fullness of time, Joe and Mary had a little boy they named Luke. They took him on the tour immediately, which meant slow driving over long bumpy roads to the next Airshow Circus performance somewhere in the mid-west. Their position was behind the rest of the circus and the flatbed truck that held their biplane. One-night, little Luke was quite sleepy, so Mary laid him down in a makeshift bed in the back of their open-air truck. It was a warm mid-summer night, and the slight breeze felt good, plus watching the fireflies in the fields as they drove made the slow-going kind of nice.

It was hours to their destination, and it was almost dawn when they stopped. Mary headed to the back of the truck and screamed! Luke was gone! Knowing he must have fallen out they got the rest of the circus performers to come help backtrack. Hours later, after knocking on doors of houses along the road, searching the grassy edges along the road, nobody had seen little Luke. Heartbroken, they turned around and went on to their destination. (This was about 100 years before cell phones, certainly no 911, no way to effectively search and find their lost child)

Several hours earlier, a dairy farmer was traveling the same road with his truck full of milk bottles to deliver to houses along the road before people awoke for breakfast. Of course, he drove slowly so as not to break any bottles, and with the windows down to catch the breeze he was surprised when he heard a baby cry. Stopping, he discovered Luke wrapped in a blanket by the side of the road. Immediately he picked him up, held him on his lap while he drove home to get his wife so they could try to find the parents. After searching for hours, they found nobody who could help or had heard of a missing child.

LET ME STOP FOR A MOMENT AND ASK: When Luke fell out of the truck, did he still have the DNA of his WING WALKER parents? How about when he was raised by the DAIRYFARMERS? Did anything change about his DNA?

Childless themselves, they decided to raise the boy as their own. The dairy farmer was a good yet strict father; and his wife was a kind and loving mother. As the boy grew, rather than assist his dad milking cows, he took special delight in climbing in the rafters of the barn, balancing high above the floor or climbing on the roof of the house and imitating the weathervane as it rotated. His mother was terrified of his antics and his father lost all patience. Punishing the boy for not keeping his feet firmly planted on the ground, he doubled his chores including milking a lot more cows each day. However, this didn't keep Luke from noticing the adjacent farm had a small airstrip behind its barn with a crop duster plane. He loved watching the plane fly over the field with his neighbor waving yet almost taunting him. O how he yearned to fly. One day he worked up courage to ask the neighbor if he could get a ride; and the neighbor obliged and in fact showed off a bit – flying over the Dairy farm and scaring the cows and angering Luke's dad. It was the best day and the worst. Luke's spirit soared and he didn't know why – he had never felt anything so exhilarating as flying! But his father was especially unimpressed, and forbade him to speak to the neighbor again, and never set foot in that plane.

Luke resigned himself to being a good dairy farmer, despite looking longingly as the neighbor flew his plane – remembering how he had felt. Until one day he was in town at the general store. There was a large poster about an Airshow Circus coming to town. His mind raced! He would have to find a way to convince his mom and dad to go to the Airshow Circus. He decided he would work harder on his chores, milk even more cows, do everything to earn approval and get them to say yes to the Airshow Circus. He certainly impressed his mom and dad, and they ended up agreeing to go to the Airshow.

Finally, the day came for the Airshow Circus. Each act was amazing! That was until the "Wing Walkers" took to the skies over the crowd. Nothing short of heart-stopping – his mom covered her eyes, his dad gasped. Luke's heart pounded as he watched Joe do the loop the loops, and Mary climb out on the wings of the biplane and then dangle from a rope swing. In his mind, he imagined doing such stunts as the Wing Walkers. He did not understand why he was thinking such thoughts.

When the Wing Walkers landed the plane, the boy ran over and began asking a million questions all about flying and walking on the wings; and could he sit in the cockpit. Joe kindly said go ahead; and was quite surprised at the enthusiasm of this young stranger. The boy quickly climbed in and then decided why not try and stand on the wings too. At about this time the Dairy-farmer and his wife walked up and began talking with the Wing Walkers. Joe asked, "is this your son"? They also commented on how enthusiastic this young man was – far above casual interest; and especially as they saw him trying to stand on the wings of the airplane.

The Dairy farmer replied to Joe that this boy was *sort of their son*; and began to tell the story of how they found him. Joe and Mary turned pale, and her lip quivered as she told the story of how their son had fallen out of their truck about 18 years ago. The Dairy farmer and his wife soon put the pieces together even down to what little Luke was wearing that fateful night. Luke was Joe and Mary's son!

Luke climbed down from the plane and ran up to his parents standing nearby with the Wing Walkers. It was an emotional time with all four parents crying together. They told Luke the truth about who he was; and he realized he had a choice to make. Would he go home with the only parents he knew, to his friends and community, and live the rest of his life as a dairy farmer or embrace the truth and discover who he was and what he was meant to be?

STOP TO THINK: What choice would you make?

He had to see what his future might hold. He went home, packed his bags, and joined the Wing Walkers as their son. It wasn't easy! The rest of the circus teens made fun of his efforts in learning to fly the plane. His clumsy way of trying to walk on the wings brought side-splitting laughter. Even with the plane on the ground and slowly being driven by his dad along the airstrip, there was no way he could master standing, much less walking on the wings. Despite his dad and mom encouraging him, and patiently teaching him everything they knew, he felt defeated, ashamed of thinking he belonged with these famous Wing Walkers! He said to himself that he belonged back on the farm; that he would be satisfied milking cows for the rest of his life.

One day, as he was hiding out from the rest of the circus folks, he was standing outside an open window where his parents sat at their kitchen table. He overheard his dad say how happy he was to have his son home; and that he didn't care if he became a Wing Walker. He loved him just the way he was. My son who was lost, is now found! His mom just smiled through her tears of joy and agreed. Luke couldn't take it – he burst in and yelled at them: "how can you love me"? I'm clumsy, I'm not like you, I'm a failure – send me back to the farm! "

His father calmly chimed in and said, "son, we love you because you are our son, not how you perform! We only push you to practice the skills we teach you, because we see in your heart there is something so special yet still hidden and won't be found unless you push yourself!" Now, Luke understood that they loved him!

The next day, Luke climbed into the cockpit and turned on the engine. It purred, almost like it expected this day to be different! It was! And every day thereafter as Luke tried new things – he was free to be himself – sure of his father's love. His talent and skills grew exponentially!

In the next year, Luke discovered his "true identity" and became an extraordinary WING WALKER! The Airshow Circus crowned Joe and Mary's son the star of the show! LUKE WING WALKER, like his mom and dad thrilled airshow audiences across the nation as he was so skillful that he almost danced across the wings of the biplane, in one death-defying stunt he crossed over between two airplanes - wing to wing as they flew side by side!

The crowd gasped and yelled with shouts of joy and admiration! Luke had discovered who he was and was living his dream!

As people in Airshow audiences across America learned Luke's story, their own unfulfilled dreams stirred within them – what if there was more in life than what they had accepted for themselves? They saw what it looked like when someone has courage to discover their "*true identity*" and then embrace their dreams.

God has a special plan and purpose for your life – what is your "true identity"?
GROUP DISCUSSION QUESTIONS:
1. What part of this story did you relate to?
2. Does what you believe about yourself change who you were created to be? Explain.
3. How does what other people say about you affect what you do?
4. When you change what you believe about yourself, what impact does that have on your life?
5. How did the WING WALKERS feel when they found their son?
6. How do you think God feels when we receive Him as our Heavenly Father?

THE TRUTH ABOUT WHAT GOD SAYS ABOUT YOU: Psalms 139:13-17 NKJV

[13] For You formed my inward parts; You covered me in my mother's womb. [14] I will praise You, for I am fearfully and wonderfully made; Marvelous are Your works, and that my soul knows very well. [15]My frame was not hidden from You, when I was made in secret, and skillfully wrought in the lowest parts of the earth. [16]Your eyes saw my substance, being yet unformed. And in Your book, they all were written, the days fashioned for me, when as yet there were none of them. [17] How precious also are Your thoughts to me, O God! How great is the sum of them!

KINGDOM ENCOUNTER
Our Group Prayer Sheet

MEMBERS:

	Name	Email	Cell Phone
1			
2			
3			
4			

Praises & Prayer Requests

"As for me, far be it from me that I should sin against the Lord by failing to pray for you." 1 Samuel 12:23

Date	Praises/Prayer Requests	Date	Answers

KINGDOM ENCOUNTER
IDENTITY - SESSION #1

I   INTRODUCTION:

The **KINGDOM OF GOD** is available to every believer by faith in the Son of God. and by the power of His Holy Spirit. When you accepted Jesus Christ as your Lord and Savior, the Holy Spirit came to live in your heart, and you acknowledged Almighty God as your heavenly Father. This was the moment of your Salvation. But there is so much more available to you. Knowing and accepting who God created you to be is central to living in HIS Kingdom now. *You are an HEIR in this Kingdom as a CHILD OF GOD* with the rights and authority that go with that title. As Christians we are taught to believe that we will live in eternity with the LORD, however, Jesus preached "repent, for the Kingdom is at hand." **(Matthew 3:2, 10:7)**. Understanding your identity and the purpose for which you were created will provide insight into how you can live "on earth as it is in heaven" **(Matthew 6:10, Luke 11:2)**, in His present Kingdom as well as the one to come upon the return of Jesus Christ.

In this session your "true identity" will unfold; you will learn that you have a unique place in God's design on earth and in His Kingdom. His plan for you originated before the beginning of time. There has never been nor will there ever be anyone like you. As a son or daughter of God you were created to have life more abundantly! **(John 10:10b)**

II   GOD SPEAKS TO YOU THROUGH HIS WORD: write out the memory verse.
A   Memory Verse: Genesis 1:27

B   Analysis Questions

1   Why do you think God created mankind in this manner?

_____

_____

_____

2   Does this change how you see yourself? Explain.

_____

_____

_____

3   If you could ask God a question about this verse, what would it be? Write it down.

_____

_____

_____

_____

III DEFINE: IDENTITY (Using Biblical resources)

_____

_____

_____

IV BIBLE STUDY
A OUR PHYSICAL/EMOTIONAL IDENTITY

1 Describe how in **Genesis 2:7** "man" was created and what caused him to come alive.

_____

_____

_____

2 In **Genesis 2:18** what did God say about man and his position on earth?

_____

_____

_____

3 According to **Genesis 2:20**, does it appear to be the case that man holds a   special place in creation? Explain your thoughts.

_____

_____

_____

4 Describe what God did in **Genesis 2:21-24**, and the significance for mankind.

_____

_____

_____

5 What does **Psalms 139:13-15** say about God's involvement in our birth after the   initial creation of Adam & Eve? How do you feel about it?

_____

_____

_____

6 In the following verses describe your value or importance to God.
   - **Luke 12:7**

_____

_____

   - **Genesis 139:17**

_____

_____

_____

_____

IV BIBLE STUDY   continued

A OUR PHYSICAL/EMOTIONAL IDENTITY   ...continue

6   In the following verses describe your value or importance to God? ...continued

- **Psalms 56:8**

_____

_____

_____

- **Psalms 139:16**

_____

_____

_____

SUMMARIZE THE MAIN THOUGHTS FROM THE VERSES IN SECTION A

B MANDATES FOR MANKIND THAT AFFECT OUR IDENTITY

1   In **Genesis 1:28** what was God's mandate for mankind?

_____

_____

2   After God's original mandate, what was the additional Instruction given to Adam (before the creation of Eve) in **Genesis 2:15-17**? Why do you think that God was so specific?

_____

_____

_____

3   Read **Genesis 3:1-16** and reflect on what happened in the Garden of Eden when Adam & Eve disregarded God's commandment and listened to the serpent (Satan). Why did they do it, what did they hope to gain? What were the consequences to mankind?

_____

_____

_____

_____

IV BIBLE STUDY   continued
B   MANDATES FOR MANKIND THAT AFFECT OUR IDENTITY   ...continued

4   In **Genesis 3:17-21** what did God do, how did that change the relationship between Himself and mankind, and how was the rest of His creation affected?

_____

_____

_____

5   Read **Genesis 3:22-24**. What did God do to set up a future redemptive plan for mankind?

_____

_____

_____

_____

6   Read the story of Noah. **Genesis 6:1-22**. What does the Bible say about how God looked at Noah in **Vs 8, in vs 9, and in vs 22**? How did that impact mankind?

_____

_____

_____

_____

7   What does God say to Noah after the flood ended in **Genesis 8:15-17**?

_____

_____

_____

8   According to **Genesis 8:20-22** what is God's mandate following the flood; what he promised to mankind (that stands to this day)?

_____

_____

_____

9   How did God change the relationship between mankind and other creatures following the flood? And what mandate for mankind did He restate to Noah? Read **Genesis 9:1-7**

_____

_____

_____

KINGDOM ENCOUNTER
IDENTITY - SESSION #1

IV BIBLE STUDY   continued
B   MANDATES FOR MANKIND THAT AFFECT OUR IDENTITY   continued

SUMMARIZE THE MAIN THOUGHTS FROM THE VERSES IN SECTION B

C   GOD CREATED YOU FOR A UNIQUE AND GOOD PURPOSE

1   How do we find purpose and success in life? Read **Matthew 6:33** and explain.

_____

_____

2   According to **Jeremiah 29:11** what is God's plan for you?

_____

_____

3   As described in **Ephesians 2:10** why did God create you and what are you supposed to do in life?

_____

_____

_____

4   **Romans 8:28** states the criteria for good outcomes in life. What is required?

_____

_____

_____

5   Regardless of our lifestyle or profession, as stated in **Matthew 28:19**, what is required of us?

_____

_____

_____

6   There are challenges in life. According to **Psalms 138:8** describe what God does for you.

_____

_____

_____

IV BIBLE STUDY   continued

C GOD CREATED YOU FOR A UNIQUE AND GOOD PURPOSE

7   What happens when you believe in Christ as promised in **Ephesians 1:13b**?

_____

_____

8   How do you find God's will and purpose for your life? Read **Romans 12:2** and explain.

_____

_____

SUMMARIZE THE MAIN THOUGHTS FROM THE VERSES IN SECTION C

D Your IDENTITY based on your relationship to Jesus Christ

1   What have you become according to **2 Corinthians 5:21**?

_____

_____

_____

2   Because of your acceptance of Christ, what has God done for you? **Read Ephesians 1:3**.

_____

_____

_____

3   According to **1 John 4:17b** describe how you are positioned in this world?

_____

_____

_____

4   The Word of God has done what for you according to **1 Peter 1:23**?

_____

_____

_____

IV   BIBLE STUDY   continued
   D   Your IDENTITY based on your relationship to Jesus Christ   ... continued
      5   Describe what has been done for you as outlined in **Ephesians 1:7**.

_____
_____
_____
_____

      6   You are complete due to your belief in Christ as your Savior. How is that stated in
          Colossians 2:9-10?

_____
_____
_____
_____

      7   What happens when you believe in Christ as promised in **Ephesians 1:13b**?

_____
_____
_____
_____

      8   The Kingdom is now, and what does it take to reign with Jesus? Read **Romans 5:17b**.

_____
_____
_____
_____

      9   Because He loves you, what does that make you according to **Romans 8:37**?

_____
_____
_____
_____

      10 What does the POWER of God do for you as described in **Colossians 1:13**?

_____
_____
_____
_____

      11 With Christ in you, what can you do? Read **Philippians 4:13** and explain.

_____
_____
_____
_____
_____

IV   BIBLE STUDY   continued

    D   Your IDENTITY based on your relationship to Jesus Christ   ...continued

SUMMARIZE THE MAIN THOUGHTS FROM THE VERSES IN SECTION D

V   SUMMARY & APPLICATION

    SUMMARY - Write out the most meaningful verse to you from each section.

A Our Physical/Emotional IDENTITY

B Mandates for mankind that affect our IDENTITY

C God created you for a unique and good purpose

D Your IDENTITY based on your relationship to Jesus Christ

APPLICATION - Think about these questions, write your thoughts if you wish to do so, or save them for class discussion.

1   Is there anything about your physical creation that makes a difference in how you see yourself?

V **APPLICATION Think about these questions, write your thoughts if you wish to do so, or save them for class discussion. ...continued**

2   Knowing that God cares about your emotional development, how does that affect our relationship to others?

_____

_____

_____

3   In God's mandates for mankind, what sticks out to you most? How does that affect how you live?

_____

_____

_____

4   Has the Holy Spirit revealed a specific plan and purpose for your life? Is it different than the life you are now living? Explain.

_____

_____

_____

5   Describe your relationship with Jesus Christ in the light of knowing your identity as an heir in His Kingdom.

_____

_____

_____

_____

NOTES

_____

_____

_____

_____

_____

_____

_____

_____

NOTES

KINGDOM ENCOUNTER

THE KINGDOM – PRESENT & FUTURE
SESSION #2

Jesus began His ministry by announcing that the Kingdom of God has come.
He also taught His disciples that He would come back
and establish a future Kingdom.

Before you begin this section ask the Holy Spirit to give you a new depth of
understanding as you read these scriptures and answer the questions.
Ask Him to give you a true **KINGDOM ENCOUNTER.**
You will discover a shift in how you see this world if you can
see yourself living in His Kingdom right now.

KINGDOM ENCOUNTER
Our Group Prayer Sheet

MEMBERS:

	Name	Email	Cell Phone
1			
2			
3			
4			

Praises & Prayer Requests

"As for me, far be it from me that I should sin against the Lord by failing to pray for you." 1 Samuel 12:23

Date	Praises/Prayer Requests	Date	Answers

KINGDOM ENCOUNTER
KINGDOM – PRESENT & FUTURE - SESSION #2

I   INTRODUCTION

Jesus began His ministry by announcing that the Kingdom of God has come, and he evidenced this by casting out demons. As He states in **Matthew 12:28** *"but if I cast out demons by the Spirit of God, surely the Kingdom of God has come upon you."*
He also taught His disciples that He would come back and establish a future Kingdom. A Kingdom that only His Father in Heaven knew of the exact timing.

Ask the Holy Spirit to give you a new depth of understanding as you read these scriptures. Ask Him to give you a true **KINGDOM ENCOUNTER**. You will see a shift in how you see this world if you can see yourself living in His Kingdom right now.

II   GOD SPEAKS TO YOU THROUGH HIS WORD: *write out the memory verse:*
A Memory Verse: MATTHEW 6:33

| |
| |
| |
| |

B ANALYSIS QUESTIONS

1   What are we supposed to seek first (above all else) and why?

_____

_____

2   Describe what you consider to be God's RIGHTEOUSNESS?

_____

_____

3   If you do the first part of this verse, what are the things you expect would be added into your life?

_____

_____

_____

4   Do you find this verse easy to apply in your life? Or do you have some issues to overcome (example: unbelief, confusion, overwhelm, questions, etc.)? Describe your feelings in either case, as the Holy Spirit may be revealing to you.

_____

_____

_____

_____

KINGDOM ENCOUNTER
KINGDOM – PRESENT & FUTURE - SESSION #2

III DEFINE: THE KINGDOM OF GOD (Using Biblical resources)

_____
_____
_____
_____

IV BIBLE STUDY

> The **KINGDOM OF GOD** has always existed as you will learn in this session. The EARTH was created as part of God's Kingdom, where mankind would have dominion and authority to be fruitful and multiply. As you learned in "**Session 1 – Identity**," when man disobeyed God and was cast out of the garden, he lost his authority, and Satan became the prince of this world. God put in motion His plan to redeem mankind in His Kingdom on Earth, with mankind as rightful heirs, as sons and daughters, in the Kingdom and under the authority of the Son of Man, Jesus Christ as Lord of Lords and King of Kings.
>
> While we see God working in the lives of men and women throughout the OLD TESTAMENT, the KINGDOM OF GOD was not mentioned as such until David became King of Israel.

A   THE KINGDOM OF GOD is first described in the **OLD TESTAMENT** by King David
(A man after God's heart)

   1   How does David describe THE KINGDOM in **1 Chronicles 29:11**?

_____
_____

   2   What is the extent of His rulership as stated in **Psalm 103:19**?

_____
_____
_____

   3   Read **Psalm 145**. A Praise of David (*and prophecy of the KINGDOM*)
   - **Verses 10-13**   What is said about the Lord and His Kingdom?

_____
_____
_____

   - **Verses 14-20** Describe what God does for those who live in His Kingdom?

_____
_____
_____

KINGDOM ENCOUNTER
KINGDOM – PRESENT & FUTURE - SESSION #2

IV BIBLE STUDY   continued

   A   THE KINGDOM OF GOD is first described in the OLD TESTAMENT   continued

SUMMARIZE THE MAIN THOUGHTS FROM THE VERSES N SECTION A

   B   THE KINGDOM OF GOD (KINGDOM OF HEAVEN) the redemption begins

   1   Matthew **3:1-12** is a world changing event. Read through, and then referring to **verses 1-2**, explain what was going on.

   _____

   _____

   2   Who was John the Baptist as described in **Isaiah 40:3** and in **Matthew 3:3**?

   _____

   _____

   3   What are the 2 types of baptisms as described in **Matthew 3:11**?

   _____

   _____

   _____

   4   In the following verses in **Matthew 3**, what was the reason Jesus insisted that John baptize him? What happened as the baptism of Jesus?
   - **Verse 15**

   _____

   _____

   - **Verse 16-17**

   _____

   _____

   5   Read **Mark 1:14-15** and describe what Jesus said was the _"gospel of the Kingdom of God?"_ What did he say specifically to the people in **verse 15**?

   _____

   _____

IV BIBLE STUDY   continued

B THE KINGDOM OF GOD (KINGDOM OF HEAVEN) the redemption begins ...continued

6   According to **Matthew 12:28** what did Jesus say was evidence that the Kingdom of God has come upon you?

_____

_____

_____

_____

7   What enabled Jesus to preach the gospel? What was his specific assignment? Read **Luke 4:18** and explain.

_____

_____

_____

_____

SUMMARIZE THE MAIN THOUGHTS FROM THE VERSES IN SECTION B

C   WHAT IS THE KINGDOM AND HOW TO ENTER IN

1   Write out the description of the **KINGDOM** as found in **Romans 14:17b**.

_____

_____

2   How does one enter the Kingdom of God as described in the following verses?
- **John 1:12-13**

_____

_____

_____

- **John 3:5-8**

_____

_____

_____

_____

IV BIBLE STUDY   continued
   C   WHAT IS THE KINGDOM AND HOW TO ENTER IN   continued

3   According to the following verses, repentance is the key to entering the Kingdom of God. What did you discover?
- **Luke 5:32**

_____

- **Acts 2:38**

_____

4   To live the Kingdom lifestyle now and reside in the Kingdom in the future one must **BELIEVE in Jesus** and the One who sent Him. How do these verses illustrate that fact?
- **John 5:24**

_____

- **John 20:30-31**

_____

- **John 3:16-17**

_____

SUMMARIZE THE MAIN THOUGHTS FROM THE VERSES IN SECTION C

D   JESUS TAUGHT IN PARABLES using everyday life situations
1   Why did Jesus teach in parables according to Matthew 13:11-17?

_____

IV BIBLE STUDY   continued

D JESUS TAUGHT IN PARABLES using everyday life situations   continued

2 Read the Parable of the Sower in **Matthew 13:3-9**, then read the explanation Jesus gave in **verses 18-23**. How would you apply this parable in your own life?

_____

_____

_____

3 Read the Parable of the Tares in **Matthew 13:24-30**. Then Jesus' explanation in **verses 37, 41-43.** Explain your takeaways.

_____

_____

_____

4 Read the Parables of the Hidden Treasure in **Matthew 13:44**, and the Pearl of Great Price in **Matthew 13:45-46**. How might that apply to you today?

_____

_____

_____

_____

SUMMARIZE THE MAIN THOUGHTS FROM THE VERSES IN SECTION D

E PRINCIPLES OF THE KINGDOM & CONSEQUENCES for rejecting them

1 Read the Parable of the Wicked Vinedressers in **Matthew 21:33-43** and answer the following questions:

- **Verse 41** What did the disciples understand?

_____

_____

- **Verse 42** What was Jesus' explanation?

_____

_____

_____

KINGDOM ENCOUNTER
KINGDOM – PRESENT & FUTURE - SESSION #2

IV BIBLE STUDY   continued

E PRINCIPLES OF THE KINGDOM & CONSEQUENCES for rejecting them   continued

1 The Parable of the Wicked Vinedressers, **Matthew 13:33-43**   ...continued

- **Verses 43-44** What are the consequences in relationship to the Kingdom of God?

_____

_____

_____

_____

2 The Parable of the Wedding in **Matthew 22:1-14**. Read and look for real-life applications in the following verses:

- **Verses 1-7**   What happened when he invited his "A-List" guests to the wedding of his son?

_____

_____

_____

_____

- **Verses 8-10**   What did he say to his servants, and what did they do?

_____

_____

_____

_____

- **Verses 11-14**   Explain what the king did and what was significant about the guest without a wedding garment? What happened to him and why?

_____

_____

_____

_____

SUMMARIZE THE MAIN THOUGHTS IN SECTION E

F LIVING IN THE KINGDOM ON EARTH

1 In **Luke 11:2-4** we find the prayer we call **"THE LORD'S PRAYER"**, which Jesus taught to His disciples. He told them that they should pray to their heavenly Father in this manner. Referring to the phrase, **"Your Kingdom come. Your will be done on earth as it is in heaven"**, how does this align with what Jesus preached, **"the Kingdom of Heaven is at hand"**?

KINGDOM ENCOUNTER
KINGDOM – PRESENT & FUTURE - SESSION #2

IV BIBLE STUDY   continued
F   LIVING IN THE KINGDOM ON EARTH   continued

1   From the previous page, in **Luke 11:24** and referring to the phrase, ***"Your Kingdom come. Your will be done on earth as it is in heaven",*** how does this align with what Jesus preached, ***"the Kingdom of Heaven is at hand"***?

_____

_____

_____

2   Read **Matthew 6:1-34**, notice that Jesus describes how we should live with one another on earth. How does the Kingdom differ from the way the world lives? Explain your thoughts.

_____

_____

_____

3   In **Matthew 5** we find important Kingdom Lifestyle choices for our life on earth while looking toward the future Kingdom of Heaven. Ask Holy Spirt revelation on life applications for you.
- **Verses 3-11**   The BEATTITUDES – How do these put life in perspective for you?

_____

_____

_____

- **Verses 17-21**   People had a misconception of what Jesus was going to do while on earth, especially in relationship to the Law and the Prophets. What did He say about following the commandments and our example to others?

_____

_____

_____

- **Verses 21-37**   Things to avoid and how to live right with others. Explain.

_____

_____

_____

- **Verses 38-48**   How should we live as a witness to others?

_____

_____

_____

IV BIBLE STUDY   continued
F LIVING IN THE KINGDOM ON EARTH   continued

4   Spiritual discernment is an important quality for believers to possess. In **1 John 4:1-3** explain what Jesus wants us to understand.

_____
_____
_____
_____

SUMMARIZE THE MAIN THOUGHTS FROM THE VERSES IN SECTION F

FUTURE KINGDOM

G PREPARATION FOR THE RETURN OF THE KING

1   Jesus told His disciples details about His return to earth. In **Matthew 24**, look for the most important points in each section.

- **Verses 4-8** Jesus wanted them to be aware of what?

_____
_____
_____

- **Verses 9-14** What must happen next, and finally culminating in **verse 14**?

_____
_____
_____

2   In **Matthew 24**, following the preliminary signs **(verses 4-14)** the Great Tribulation occurs. Read **Verses 15-28**. State God's plan for His elect people, found in verses **21-22**:

_____
_____
_____

KINGDOM ENCOUNTER
KINGDOM – PRESENT & FUTURE - SESSION #2

IV BIBLE STUDY   continued
G   PREPARATION FOR THE RETURN OF THE KING   continued

3   After the Great Tribulation, Jesus comes back. Refer to the following verses in **Matthew 24**:

- **Verse 30** Describe how Jesus returns to earth, and how that affects people on earth.

_____

- **Verse 31** Who is gathered to accompany Jesus? Where do they come from?

_____

SUMMARIZE THE MAIN THOUGHTS FROM THE VERSES IN SECTION G

H   DAY OF THE LORD as described by these Old Testament Prophets

1   What GOD plans for the earth at the end of time as we know it is described in **Zephaniah 3:8-9**. In **verse 9** He speaks of restoration – explain.

_____

2   Ultimate end-time fulfilment of God's promises to mankind is found in **Isaiah 35:4-10**.
- **Verse 4**   State the hope found for the "fearful-hearted.

_____

- **Verse 10**   What happens after they win the victory in battle?

_____

KINGDOM ENCOUNTER
KINGDOM – PRESENT & FUTURE - SESSION #2

IV BIBLE STUDY   continued

H   DAY OF THE LORD as described by these Old Testament Prophets   continued

3   **Isaiah 66** describes not only the inclusion of the Gentiles but what will happen to earth. Ask the Holy Spirit to show you how we should understand these times.

- **Verses 19-21**   Describe God's actions.

_____

_____

_____

_____

_____

- **Verses 22-24**   How does God set up His final Kingdom?

_____

_____

_____

_____

4   **Zechariah 14:1-15**   Describes **THE DAY OF THE LORD**. Write down the most important points about what happens to the people of earth during this time. Describe how the believers are affected.

_____

_____

_____

_____

SUMMARIZE THE MAIN THOUGHTS FROM THE VERSES IN SECTION H

I   KING OF KINGS AND LORD OF LORDS – THE FINAL KINGDOM

While there is disagreement among many learned theologians as to when or if a "rapture" of the saints occurs, when tribulation begins and ends, and other facets of our Christian faith; all followers of Jesus Christ agree that there is an end of time when He comes back to earth to reign as King of Kings and Lord of Lords. The **KINGDOM ENCOUNTER** discipleship will cover the very end (not whether we may personally be on earth to witness it) when Christ is seen by all mankind in the clouds and returns to earth to reign for eternity. Let the scriptures guide you.

IV BIBLE STUDY   continued
I KING OF KINGS AND LORD OF LORDS – THE FINAL KINGDOM

1 **Revelation 19:11-21** describes the moment when Jesus comes back. Describe your findings in the following verses:

- **Verses 13-16**   What was He called? Describe those who came with Him. What was written on His thigh?

- **Verses 19-21**   Who made up the opposing army? What happened to them?

2 After the Lord and His army defeated His enemies, **Revelation 20:1-3** states what happens to Satan. Describe.

3 The Saints reign with Christ 1000 years. Read **Revelation 20:4-6.** Answer the following questions:

- **Verse 4** Who were those who reign with Christ?

- **Verse 5** What is significant about the people in this verse?

- **Verse 6** What is significant about the first resurrection?

IV BIBLE STUDY   continued

I   KING OF KINGS AND LORD OF LORDS – THE FINAL KINGDOM   continued

4   At the end of 1000 years, Satan is released. **Revelation 20:7-10** describes the final battle.

- **Verse 8** What does Satan do to prepare for battle? Who is involved?

_____

_____

_____

- **Verse 9-10** Who won and how did the battle unfold? What happens to Satan?

_____

_____

_____

_____

_____

THE FINAL JUDGMENT

As we learned in #3 above, the saints were part of the first resurrection. **The GREAT WHITE THRONE JUDGMENT** is for the dead who are raised at this second resurrection.

Describe what occurs at the **JUDGMENT** as explained in **Revelation 20:11-15**. Who is cast into the Lake of Fire?

_____

_____

_____

_____

_____

_____

LIFE IN THE FINAL KINGDOM

1   **Revelation 21:1** gives a glimpse of this KINGDOM – describe. What has changed?

_____

_____

_____

_____

_____

KINGDOM ENCOUNTER
KINGDOM – PRESENT & FUTURE - SESSION #2

IV BIBLE STUDY   continued
I KING OF KINGS AND LORD OF LORDS – THE FINAL KINGDOM   continued
LIFE IN THE FINAL KINGDOM   ...continued

2   Read **Revelation 21:2-27**   This is John's description of the Kingdom and the New Jerusalem.
- **Verses 2, and 10-22** Describe the tabernacle of God, the Holy City, and what seems most significant to you?

_____

_____

_____

_____

_____

- **Verses 3-4** What will the Lord do for His people?

_____

_____

_____

_____

- **Verses 5-8** What was John told?

_____

_____

_____

_____

- **Verses 23-26** What was unique about the city? Who gets to enter and what do they bring with them?

_____

_____

_____

_____

- **Verse 27** There are some who are excluded from the city, who are they? What is required to enter the city?

_____

_____

_____

_____

KINGDOM ENCOUNTER
KINGDOM – PRESENT & FUTURE - SESSION #2

IV BIBLE STUDY   continued
I   KING OF KINGS AND LORD OF LORDS – THE FINAL KINGDOM   continued
LIFE IN THE FINAL KINGDOM

3   What will life be like in the **KINGDOM OF GOD** on earth as described in **Revelation 22:1-5?**

_____
_____
_____
_____

4   What are the important points in these verses in **Revelation 22**?   Read each selection of verses and explain your findings:
- **Verse 7**   Who is blessed?

_____
_____

- **Verses 10-11**   What did the angel tell John?

_____
_____
_____

- **Verse 12**   What is Jesus bringing with Him? Why is this important?

_____
_____
_____

- **Verse 14-15**   The blessed and the cursed

_____
_____
_____

- **Verses 16-19**   Life advice and dire warnings

_____
_____
_____

- **Verse 20**   The final words of Jesus – your thoughts

_____
_____

KINGDOM ENCOUNTER
KINGDOM – PRESENT & FUTURE - SESSION #2

V SUMMARY & APPLICATION

SUMMARY – Write out the verse that is most meaningful to you from each section.

A THE KINGDOM OF GOD is first described in the OLD TESTAMENT
B THE KINGDOM OF GOD (KINGDOM OF HEAVEN) – the redemption begins
C WHAT IS THE KINGDOM AND HOW TO ENTER IN
D JESUS TAUGHT IN PARABLES
E PRINCIPLES OF THE KINGDOM AND CONSEQUENCES for rejecting them
F LIVING IN THE KINGDOM ON EARTH
G PREPARATION FOR THE RETURN OF THE KING
H DAY OF THE LORD
I KING OF KINGS AND LORD OF LORDS – THE FINAL KINGDOM

APPLICATION – think about these questions, write your thoughts if you wish to do so, or save them for discussion in your small group.

1 What has the Holy Spirit revealed to you about living in the Kingdom of God on earth?

_____

_____

2 What about living a Kingdom Lifestyle do you find most challenging?

_____

_____

_____

NOTES

KINGDOM ENCOUNTER
KINGDOM – PRESENT & FUTURE - SESSION #2

NOTES

KINGDOM ENCOUNTER

THE HOLY SPIRIT
SESSION #3

As you invite the HOLY SPIRIT to speak to you through this session,
you will realize that His Spirit testifies with your spirit that you are His son or daughter,
and an heir in the Kingdom of God. (Romans 8:16-17)
Just as Jesus promised to His disciples, so He intends for you.

KINGDOM ENCOUNTER
Our Group Prayer Sheet

MEMBERS:

	Name	Email	Cell Phone
1			
2			
3			
4			

Praises & Prayer Requests

"As for me, far be it from me that I should sin against the Lord by failing to pray for you." 1 Samuel 12:23

Date	Praises/Prayer Requests	Date	Answers

KINGDOM ENCOUNTER
HOLY SPIRIT - SESSION #3

I   INTRODUCTION:

Jesus now sits at the right hand of God the Father in Heaven. In this session you will come to know at a much deeper level the One whom Jesus promised that His Father would send – *"But the Helper, the Holy Spirit, whom the Father will send in My name, He will teach you all things, and bring to your remembrance all things that I said to you." NKJV*

As you invite the **HOLY SPIRIT** to speak to you through this session, you will realize that **His Spirit** testifies with your spirit that you are his son or daughter, and an heir in the **Kingdom of God. (Romans 8:16-17)** Just as Jesus promised to His disciples, so He intends for you.

II   GOD SPEAKS TO YOU THROUGH HIS WORD: write out the memory verse.
A   MEMORY VERSE: John 14:15-17

| |
| |
| |
| |

B   Analysis Questions

1   What does Jesus do (for His disciples, and applies to us) for those who love Him and keep His commandments?

_____

_____

2   In **verse 17**, what does Jesus call Him who the world cannot receive?

_____

_____

_____

3   Why doesn't the world know the One Jesus sends?

_____

_____

_____

4   Jesus explained how the disciples would know Him according to the way He would interact with them. Describe.

_____

_____

_____

_____

_____

III DEFINE: THE HOLY SPIRIT (Using Biblical resources)

_____

_____

_____

_____

IV BIBLE STUDY

A THE NATURE AND PERSON OF THE HOLY SPIRIT

1 Only the third person of the Trinity, The Holy Spirit, provides certain spiritual abilities to believers. Read **1 Corinthians 12:3-6** and describe what He does for us.

_____

_____

_____

2 In **2 Corinthians 13:14**, the nature of each person of the Trinity is described; what is ascribed to the Holy Spirit?

_____

_____

3 What does the Holy Spirit specifically do for believers? Read **Romans 8:26-27** and describe.

_____

_____

_____

4 Describe the different aspects of the Divine nature of the Holy Spirit in the following verses:
   - **Psalms 139:7-12**

_____

_____

   - **1 Corinthians 2:10-11**

_____

_____

_____

   - **Hebrews 9:14**

_____

_____

_____

_____

KINGDOM ENCOUNTER
HOLY SPIRIT - SESSION #3

IV BIBLE STUDY   continued
A THE NATURE AND PERSON OF THE HOLY SPIRIT   continued

5   In the following verses, describe the work of the Holy Spirit regarding salvation.

- **John 16:7-8**

_____
_____
_____
_____

- **John 6:63**

_____
_____
_____

- **Matthew 12:31-32**

_____
_____
_____

- **John 3:1-8**

_____
_____
_____
_____

SUMMARIZE THE MAIN THOUGHTS FROM THE VERSES IN SECTION A

B   THE HOLY SPIRIT IN THE OLD TESTAMENT – He is God, and the Third Person of the Trinity. He was referred to by various names: Spirit of God, Spirit of the Lord, or the Spirit.   He was not called the "Holy Spirit" in the Old Testament.

1   What was the Spirit doing in **Genesis 1:1-2**? What does this tell you about His importance?

_____
_____
_____
_____

IV BIBLE STUDY   continued

B THE HOLY SPIRIT IN THE OLD TESTAMENT – He is God, and the Third Person of the Trinity.   ...continued

2   Read the story of Joseph and how he deciphered Pharaoh's dream – which would bring famine to Egypt. **Genesis 41:33-42**. Pharaoh recognized what about Joseph in **verses 38 and 39**?

_____

_____

_____

3   Describe how these Old Testament leaders were anointed and empowered by the Holy Spirit as outlined in these verses?
   - **2 Samuel 23:1-2   DAVID**

_____

_____

   - **Numbers 11:17   MOSES**

_____

_____

   - **Numbers 27:18   JOSHUA**

_____

_____

   - **Judges 6:34   GIDEON**

_____

_____

   - **2 Chronicles 24:20   ZECHARIAH**

_____

_____

IV BIBLE STUDY   continued

B   THE HOLY SPIRIT IN THE OLD TESTAMENT – He is God, and the Third Person of the Trinity.   ...continued

4   In **Nehemiah 9:19-20** describe what the Spirit did for God's people in the wilderness.

_____
_____
_____

5   Who is speaking through the prophet Isaiah in **Isaiah 48:16**? How does this validate a "Triune God?"

_____
_____
_____

6   What did King David ask of God in relationship to the Holy Spirit in **Psalm 51:10-12**? How might this impact your own life?

_____
_____
_____

7   Before the coming of the great and awesome day of the Lord, what does **Joel:2:28-29** say regarding the Spirit?

_____
_____
_____
_____

SUMMARIZE THE MAIN THOUGHTS FROM THE VERSES IN SECTION B

C   THE HOLY SPIRIT IN THE NEW TESTAMENT – special assignments

1   What assignment did the Holy Spirit have regarding John the Baptist? Read **Luke 1:15**

_____
_____
_____

IV BIBLE STUDY   continued
C   THE HOLY SPIRIT IN THE NEW TESTAMENT – special assignments   continued

2   In **Luke 1:35** what life-changing moment was about to happen? Describe.

_____

_____

_____

_____

3   By the actions of the Holy Spirit in **Matthew 3:16-17**, what do you think are the most significant takeaways?

_____

_____

_____

4   In **Matthew 4:1** Jesus was led "by the Spirit" into the wilderness to be tempted by the devil. What is the Holy Spirit revealing to you would be some the reasons God would allow this to happen to His son? What did Satan hope to accomplish?

_____

_____

_____

_____

_____

5   **Romans 1:3-4**   According to verse 4, why did the "Spirit of holiness" declare Jesus to be the "Son of God with power"?

_____

_____

_____

6   Although Jesus was speaking to His disciples, what he said is applicable to us today. Read **John 14:26** and describe the benefits for us.

_____

_____

_____

7   According to **Acts 9:31** what characteristics did the churches have? Describe why they were multiplied. (Applicable for church multiplication today)

_____

_____

_____

KINGDOM ENCOUNTER
HOLY SPIRIT - SESSION #3

IV BIBLE STUDY   continued
C   THE HOLY SPIRIT IN THE NEW TESTAMENT – special assignments   continued

8   **Acts 16:6-7** describes an important aspect of listening to and following the Holy Spirit. What did He do? How might that help us today?

_____

_____

_____

9   Where does the Holy Spirit reside and why is that important as explained in **1 Corinthians 6:19-20?**

_____

_____

_____

_____

SUMMARIZE THE MAIN THOUGHTS FROM THE VERSES IN SECTION C

D   RECEIVING THE HOLY SPIRIT – the process of regeneration

Conversion – turning to God – includes repentance, faith in Jesus, forgiveness of sins, baptism in water and receiving the Holy Spirit. It can happen instantly or take a lifetime.

1   To see the Kingdom of God what must one do? **Read John 3:3.**

_____

_____

2   God's will for us goes much deeper than just seeing the Kingdom. Explain what His will is for us in **John 3:5-7**

_____

_____

_____

_____

KINGDOM ENCOUNTER
HOLY SPIRIT - SESSION #3

IV BIBLE STUDY   continued
D RECEIVING THE HOLY SPIRIT – the process of regeneration   continued

3 The Holy Spirit enables us to know His Kingdom apart from the spirit of this world. To discern spiritual matters. Read **1 Corinthians 2:10-14** and describe the benefits for us.

_____

_____

_____

_____

SUMMARIZE THE MAIN THOUGHTS FROM THE VERSES IN SECTION D

E JESUS BAPTIZES WITH THE HOLY SPIRIT

> The fullness of God (the Father, the Son, and the Holy Spirit) is available to every believer when one receives salvation. However, the experience we know as the "Baptism with/of/in the Holy Spirit" can happen at the same time one is saved or as a later event in a believer's life. Oftentimes, it occurs once one realizes there is more to know, at a deeper level, in developing a powerful relationship with our Lord Jesus Christ and asks God for the Baptism of the Holy Spirit.
>
> The actual baptism of the Holy Spirit is described by some as a "power surge" that affects both the physical and mental being; and in other people it is a sense of overwhelming love, peace, and joy. Either way it is a life-changing moment when **you know that you know** how much your heavenly Father loves you and pours His Spirit into your total being.

1 What does **Luke 11:13** say about how to receive the Holy Spirit?

_____

_____

2 In **Mark, Matthew, and Luke** (3 of the 4 gospels), what did John say about his assignment and the ONE who would come after him:

- **Mark 1:8**

_____

_____

_____

_____

IV BIBLE STUDY   continued
E   JESUS BAPTIZES WITH THE HOLY SPIRIT   continued

2   In **Mark, Matthew, and Luke** (3 of the 4 gospels), what did John say about his assignment and the ONE who would come after him: ...continued from previous page

- **Matthew 3:11**

_____

_____

- **Luke 3:16**

_____

_____

3   Explain what John the Baptist said **about the one** who told him to baptize with water. Read **John 1:33** for your answer.

_____

_____

_____

4   Jesus Christ, before he ascended to the Father, told his disciples they were about to receive the PROMISE OF THE FATHER. Read the following verses and explain.

- **Acts 1:4-5**

_____

_____

_____

- **Acts 1:8**

_____

_____

_____

_____

5   **THE DAY JESUS HAD PROMISED – would mean everything to the world!**
The Day of Pentecost had fully come, they were all in one accord in one place. (Acts 2:1)
Refer to verses below and answer the questions.

- **Acts 2:2** Give the details of what they experienced.

_____

_____

_____

- **Acts 2:3** What specifically happened to those present?

_____

_____

_____

_____

IV BIBLE STUDY   continued
E   JESUS BAPTIZES WITH THE HOLY SPIRIT   continued

6   On the Day of Pentecost, 3 things happened when those in the upper room were filled with the **HOLY SPIRIT**. **Acts 2:4 In the** <u>**Amplified Version**</u> —

There are 3 specific things that happened as stated in **Acts 2:4** (Amplified Version)

1)   And they were all filled (that is, diffused throughout their being) with the Holy Spirit.
2)   And began to speak in other tongues (different languages)
3)   As the Spirit was giving them the ability to speak out (clearly and appropriately)

•   What was the specific action of the **HOLY SPIRIT** in #3?   Does this make a difference in what you believe about *"speaking in tongues"*?

_____
_____
_____
_____

7   There are 2 types of baptisms. Paul explains the difference to a group of 12 Gentiles — describe your findings in **Acts 19:2-7.**

_____
_____
_____
_____
_____
_____
_____

SUMMARIZE THE MAIN THOUGHTS FROM THE VERSES IN SECTION E

F   THE GIFTS OF THE HOLY SPIRIT

1   Describe what is provided to believers according to **1 Corinthians 12:4-6.**

_____
_____
_____
_____
_____

IV BIBLE STUDY   continued

F THE GIFTS OF THE HOLY SPIRIT

2 **1 Corinthians 12:7** states that "... the manifestation of the Spirit, which is given to each one for the profit of all?" List the gifts of the Spirit found in **1 Corinthians 12:8-10**.

_____

_____

_____

_____

3 What is unique about the gifts as stated in **1 Corinthians 12:11**?

_____

_____

_____

4 What is the purpose of the Gifts of the Holy Spirit for the church as outlined by Apostle Paul in **1 Corinthians 12:27-31?**

_____

_____

_____

5 Reflect on what Paul states is the "more excellent way" (**verse 31 above**) in describing the use of the Gifts as found in **1 Corinthians 13:1-3**. What is it?

_____

_____

SUMMARIZE THE MAIN THOUGHTS FROM THE VERSES IN SECTION F

G THE GIFT OF TONGUES

The Holy Spirit operates in every believer and throughout the various church ministries. God gives us the ability to speak in tongues, but we get to choose when to speak or keep silent. He does not force anyone to speak in tongues. It does not mean we do not have the Holy Spirit, nor are we ineffective in ministry if we do not use this gift.

IV BIBLE STUDY   continued
G THE GIFT OF TONGUES   continued

1 God appointed many aspects of church life which are available to all believers. Read **1 Corinthians 12:28** and explain your findings.

_____

_____

_____

_____

2 Here are 5 accounts of baptism with the Holy Spirit. Notice whether the speaking in tongues occurred. Describe each water baptism & whether the individual received the gift of tongues at the same time.

- **Acts 2:4**

_____

_____

_____

- **Acts 8:14-17**

_____

_____

_____

- **Acts 9:17-18**

_____

_____

_____

- **Acts 10:44**

_____

_____

_____

- **Acts 19:1-7**

_____

_____

_____

_____

IV BIBLE STUDY   continued
G   THE GIFT OF TONGUES

3 The Gift of Tongues has two important functions.
First – **PERSONAL EDIFICATION** – to build up the inner man, providing peace and calm.
Second – **PUBLIC EXHORTATION –** to bring a Word from God

In this section we will explore both aspects of the GIFT OF TONGUES.

FIRST – PERSONAL EDIFICATION
➢ This type of tongue is unknown to the speaker and is often called a "prayer language." It does not require interpretation because it is only for personal benefit.
➢ In a corporate setting, the pastor may invite personal "prayer languages" to be spoken in the congregation for a specific purpose and limited duration. In this case no interpreter is required.

- What does this type of tongue do for a believer as found in **1 Corinthians 14:4a**? If you currently speak in tongues, do you find this an important aspect of your prayer life?

_____
_____
_____

- What is a believer encouraged to do as stated in **Jude 1:20**?

_____
_____
_____

- What is suggested in relationship to the use of tongues as described in **1 Corinthians 14:15?**

_____
_____
_____
_____

SECOND – PUBLIC EXHORTATION
➢ A Tongue that is a known language, but unknown to the speaker. What occurred at Pentecost.
➢ If the Tongue is an unknown language the scriptures state that it must be interpreted. The Gift of Interpretation of Tongues is also a Gift of the Holy Spirit.

IV BIBLE STUDY   continued

G   THE GIFT OF TONGUES   continued

3   The Gift of Tongues has two important functions, Personal Edification, and Public Exhortation.   ...continued

- What are signs that follow believers as described in **Mark 16:17-20?**

_____

_____

_____

- In **1 Corinthians, Chapter 14** the apostle Paul explains the appropriate use of tongues in the church. Summarize your thoughts in each verse below:

  ➢ **1 Corinthians 14:5**

_____

_____

  ➢ **1 Corinthians 14:13-14**

_____

_____

_____

_____

  ➢ **1 Corinthians 14:18-19**

_____

_____

_____

  ➢ **1 Corinthians 14:26**

_____

_____

_____

  ➢ **1 Corinthians 14:39-40**

_____

_____

_____

SUMMARIZE THE MAIN THOUGHTS FROM THE VERSES IN SECTION G

V SUMMARY & APPLICATION

SUMMARY – Write out the verse that is most meaningful to you from each section in the study.

A THE NATURE AND PERSON OF THE HOLY SPIRIT
B THE HOLY SPIRIT IN THE OLD TESTAMENT
C THE HOLY SPIRIT IN THE NEW TESTAMENT
D RECEIVING THE HOLY SPIRIT
E JESUS BAPTIZES WITH THE HOLY SPIRIT
F THE GIFTS OF THE HOLY SPIRIT
G THE GIFT OF TONGUES

APPLICATION – think about these questions, write your thoughts if you wish to do so, or save them for discussion in your small group.

1   What did you learn about the Holy Spirit that you did not know before?

V SUMMARY & APPLICATION   continued
APPLICATION   continued

2   Has your relationship with the Holy Spirit changed during this session? If so, in what ways?

_____
_____
_____
_____

3   Do you see the Kingdom of God any differently due to what you have learned about the Holy Spirit?

_____
_____
_____
_____

4   What is most valuable to you about your relationship with the Holy Spirit?

_____
_____
_____

5   Is there any section in this Session the especially spoke to you? Explain.

_____
_____
_____
_____

NOTES

_____
_____
_____
_____
_____
_____
_____

NOTES

KINGDOM ENCOUNTER

THE WORD
SESSION #4

The Bible is THE WORD OF GOD and our manual for living in GOD'S KINGDOM. Even if you have read the Bible many times, and think you know it well; as you complete these pages, invite the Holy Spirit to do a NEW THING in your heart.

KINGDOM ENCOUNTER
Our Group Prayer Sheet

MEMBERS:

	Name	Email	Cell Phone
1			
2			
3			
4			

Praises & Prayer Requests

"As for me, far be it from me that I should sin against the Lord by failing to pray for you." 1 Samuel 12:23

Date	Praises/Prayer Requests	Date	Answers

KINGDOM ENCOUNTER
THE WORD – SESSION #4

I INTRODUCTION

The **Bible** is **THE WORD OF GOD** and our manual for living in **GOD'S KINGDOM**. Even if you have read the Bible many times, and think you know it well; as you complete these pages, invite the **Holy Spirit** to do a **NEW THING** in your heart.

GOD brings His message to you based on two Greek words. The **LOGOS**, which is the written **WORD of GOD** recorded in the Bible; and the **RHEMA**, which is the instant, personal communication from **GOD** through **HIS WORD** but directly to you. This takes place when you read a passage and know it's meant for you – especially when you've read it before a thousand times – but this time it jumps off the page. That's **RHEMA Word**!

Dig for the gold, the **RHEMA Word** which will transform your life even as you read and let it soak into your soul. The **RHEMA** is straight from **GOD'S HEART**, brought by the **HOLY SPIRIT** specifically for you.

II GOD SPEAKS TO YOU THROUGH HIS WORD: write out the memory verse.
A Memory Verse: Hebrews 4:12

B ANALYSIS QUESTIONS

1   The **WORD OF GOD** is not dead! Describe the first 2 attributes in this verse. What does this mean to you?

2   What are the implications of the **WORD OF GOD** being "Sharper than a double-edged sword?"

3   What does the **WORD OF GOD** do in relationship to your heart?

4   How does understanding this verse change your connection to the **WORD OF GOD**?

KINGDOM ENCOUNTER
THE WORD – SESSION #4

III DEFINE: THE WORD (Using Biblical resources)

_____
_____
_____
_____

IV BIBLE STUDY

  A THE NATURE OF GOD'S WORD

    1 In the following verses, if possible, using the **_NIV or the Passion translation_** (for a greater sense of context) describe what is most meaningful to you?

       • **2 Timothy 3:16**

_____
_____
_____

       • **1 Thessalonians 2:13**

_____
_____
_____

    2 What does the Holy Spirit do for us in relationship to His Word as described in **1 Corinthians 2:12-13.**

_____
_____
_____
_____

    3 Regarding the Word of God, what was unique as found in **Exodus 31:18**?

_____
_____
_____

    4 What did you learn about the Word of God in **2 Samuel 22:31**?

_____
_____

    5 How does time affect God's Word according to **Matthew 24:35**?

_____
_____
_____

KINGDOM ENCOUNTER
THE WORD – SESSION #4

IV BIBLE STUDY   continued
  A   THE NATURE OF GOD'S WORD   continued
  6   What will the "Holy Scriptures" do for you according to **2 Timothy 3:15**?

_____
_____
_____

SUMMARIZE THE MAIN THOUGHTS FROM THE VERSES IN SECTION A

  B   THE POWER OF GOD'S WORD
  1   What was the ultimate power of God's Word as described in **Psalms 33:6**?

_____
_____

  2   How are husbands to love their wives, and what are the results as described in **Ephesians 5:25-26**?

_____
_____
_____

  3   According to **Romans 1:16** how does the Word assure a believer of salvation?

_____
_____
_____

  4   What does the Word of God do in a believer's life as described in the following verses:
  • **Proverbs 30:5-6**

_____
_____
_____

  • **Psalms 119:105**

_____
_____
_____

KINGDOM ENCOUNTER
THE WORD – SESSION #4

IV BIBLE STUDY   continued
B   THE POWER OF GOD'S WORD   continued

5   As it is written in **Hebrews 4:12** what does the Word of God do to a believer's heart and attitudes?

_____
_____
_____
_____

6   Explain the use of these 2 pieces of armor and the relationship to the Word of God as found in **Ephesians 6:17.**

_____
_____
_____
_____

SUMMARIZE THE MAIN THOUGHTS FROM THE VERSES IN SECTION B

_____
_____
_____
_____
_____
_____

C   THE CENTRAL PERSON OF THE BIBLE

1   In the following verses, how does the Word point to Jesus?

- **John 1:1-2**

_____
_____
_____

- **John 1:14**

_____
_____
_____

- **Acts 18:28**

_____
_____
_____
_____

IV BIBLE STUDY   continued
C   THE CENTRAL PERSON OF THE BIBLE   continued

1   In the following verses, how does the Word point to Jesus?   ...continued

- **1 John 1:1**

_____

_____

_____

_____

- **Luke 24:44**

_____

_____

_____

_____

SUMMARIZE THE MAIN THOUGHTS FROM THE VERSES IN SECTION C

D   HOW DOES GOD'S WORD IMPACT YOUR LIFE?

In the following verses ask the Holy Spirit to reveal to you the most important aspects for Kingdom living and state your findings.

- **Psalms 119:16**

_____

_____

- **Romans 15:4**

_____

_____

_____

- **Acts 17:11**

_____

_____

_____

- **James 1:22**

_____

_____

_____

KINGDOM ENCOUNTER
THE WORD – SESSION #4

IV BIBLE STUDY   continued
D   HOW DOES GOD'S WORD IMPACT YOUR LIFE?   continued
In the following verses ask the Holy Spirit to reveal to you the most important aspects for Kingdom living and state your findings.   ...continued
- **Matthew 4:4**

_____

_____

- **2 Timothy 2:15**

_____

_____

SUMMARIZE THE MAIN THOUGHTS FROM THE VERSES IN SECTION D

E   KINGDOM LIFESTYLE
By reading **THE WORD** in these verses, what do you find that will help you live a **Kingdom Lifestyle**?
- **Jeremiah 9:24**

_____

_____

- **Psalms 40:8**

_____

_____

- **Isaiah 55:11**

_____

_____

- **2 Peter 1:2-4**

_____

_____

_____

IV BIBLE STUDY   continued
E   KINGDOM LIFESTYLE   continued

By reading **THE WORD** in these verses, what do you find that will help you live a **Kingdom Lifestyle?** ...continued

- **Revelation 1:3**

_____

_____

- **Psalms 119:9**

_____

_____

- **Romans 10:17**

_____

_____

SUMMARIZE THE MAIN THOUGHTS FROM THE VERSES IN SECTION E

F   WHAT HAPPENS IF WE DON'T KNOW OR IGNORE GOD'S WORD?

1   How does one keep from sin according to **Psalms 119:11**?

_____

_____

2   According to **2 Timothy 4:3-4**, what will men do who do not accept sound doctrine?

_____

_____

3   In **Matthew 22:29** how did Jesus respond to people not knowing Scripture?

_____

_____

_____

KINGDOM ENCOUNTER
THE WORD – SESSION #4

IV BIBLE STUDY   continued
F   WHAT HAPPENS IF WE DON'T KNOW OR IGNORE GOD'S WORD?   Continued

4   What does **Proverbs 1:8-31** say about why God may not answer when some people pray?

_____

_____

5   According to **Jeremiah 6:19**, what will happen to those who do not listen to the Word of God?

_____

_____

_____

SUMMARIZE THE MAIN THOUGHTS FROM THE VERSES IN SECTION F

V   SUMMARY & APPLICATION
SUMMARY – Write out the verse that is most meaningful to you from each section in this study.

A   THE NATURE OF GOD'S WORD

B   THE POWER OF GOD'S WORD

C   THE CENTRAL PERSON OF THE BIBLE

D   HOW DOES GOD'S WORD IMPACT YOUR LIFE

V SUMMARY & APPLICATION   continued

SUMMARY – Write out the verse that is most meaningful to you from each section in this study.   ...continued

E KINGDOM LIFESTYLE
F WHAT HAPPENS IF WE DON'T KNOW OR IGNORE GOD'S WORD

APPLICATION – think about these questions, write your thoughts if you wish to do so, or save them for discussion in your small group.

1 What have you learned in this session that was a **NEW THING** regarding the **WORD OF GOD**?

_____

_____

_____

2 Was there a specific **RHEMA WORD** that you received in this session? Explain how that might impact your life?

_____

_____

_____

3 How will these lessons help you live a **KINGDOM OF GOD LIFESTYLE** right now?

_____

_____

_____

_____

NOTES

_____

_____

_____

_____

_____

NOTES

NOTES

KINGDOM ENCOUNTER

TEMPTATION & TRIALS
SESSION #5

In this session the Holy Spirit will guide you through practical ways
to achieve victory when faced with Life's challenges.
You will learn that TEMPTATION does not come from God,
but it is allowed by Him; and that TRIALS may come from God
to test and strengthen your faith. TRIALS also come from the devil,
people in your life, the world we live in,
and is often a result of the choices we make.

KINGDOM ENCOUNTER
Our Group Prayer Sheet

MEMBERS:

	Name	Email	Cell Phone
1			
2			
3			
4			

Praises & Prayer Requests

"As for me, far be it from me that I should sin against the Lord by failing to pray for you." 1 Samuel 12:23

Date	Praises/Prayer Requests	Date	Answers

KINGDOM ENCOUNTER
TEMPTATION & TRIALS – SESSION #5

I INTRODUCTION:

   In this life we have tribulation, the good news is that Jesus Christ has overcome the world! In this session the Holy Spirit will guide you through practical ways to achieve victory when faced with Life's challenges. You will learn that **TEMPTATION *does not* come from God**, but it is allowed by Him; and that **TRIALS may come from God** to test and strengthen your faith. **TRIALS** also come from the devil, people in your life, the world we live in, and is often a result of the choices we make. We cannot prevent every challenge that comes our way, but we can control our reaction to it. The Bible provides a roadmap for your victory and a **Kingdom of God Lifestyle** is your reward!

II GOD SPEAKS TO YOU THROUGH HIS WORD: *write out the memory verse.*

   A Memory Verse: 1 Corinthians 10:13

   B Analysis Questions:

   1 Is there any temptation that should take you by surprise? Explain

   2 What helps you to face temptation in your life?

   3 What does God do on our behalf when he allows us to face temptation in our life?

   4 What do you do when you are faced with temptation and you feel it is overwhelming, or about to get the best of you?

KINGDOM ENCOUNTER
TEMPTATION & TRIALS – SESSION #5

III DEFINE: TEMPTATION & TRIALS (Using Biblical resources)
- **TEMPTATION:**

_____

_____

- **TRIALS:**

_____

_____

IV BIBLE STUDY
A NATURE OF TEMPTATION
1   Who or what is responsible for temptation in our life from the following verses?
- **James 1:13-14**
    - ➤ **Verse 13** What does this say about GOD as the responsible party?

_____

_____

    - ➤ **Verse 14** What is an important factor about temptation?

_____

_____

- **1 John 2:16** Describe the areas of temptation and in what ways we are affected?

_____

_____

_____

Galatians 5:17 - talks about the **FLESH** and the **SPIRIT** (the **HOLY SPIRIT**). (In the **"NATURAL",** the **"FLESH"** is our **"body";** however, our **"FLESH"** in the **"spiritual"** sense is more than our body, and has to do with satisfying a wide range of desires. The **"FLESH"** is under the control of our **"MIND"** which is part of our *SOUL – the Mind, the Will, and the Emotions.*)

- From **Galatians 5:17**, what problem occurs when the **"MIND"** causes our **"FLESH/BODY"** to act contrary to the leading of the **SPIRIT OF GOD**?

_____

_____

2   How does one recognize temptation and what must we do to overcome and/or avoid the trap it brings to our life? Read **Romans 7:21-23** and explain.

_____

_____

SUMMARIZE THE MAIN THOUGHTS FROM THE VERSES IN SECTION A

IV BIBLE STUDY continued

B HOW DO PEOPLE GET CAUGHT IN TEMPTATION?

1 Read the following verses and describe your findings:
- **Proverbs 11:6**

_____

_____

_____

2 Read **2 Samuel 11:1-17** and answer the questions regarding this situation in the life of King David.
- **Verses 1-2** Why did David find himself in a position to be tempted?

_____

_____

_____

- **Verses 3-5** Describe the consequences of yielding to temptation.

_____

_____

_____

- **Verses 6-13** Describe David's attempt to right the situation.

_____

_____

_____

- **Verses 14-17** What did David decide to do? Was that his only option?

_____

_____

_____

3 According to **1 Corinthians 7:3-5** how should couples protect their marriage against temptation?

_____

_____

_____

_____

4 **Galatians 5:19-21** describes **"works of the flesh"** (Remember, the **MIND** controls the **FLESH**, so these are **Soul issues** – the mind, the will, and emotions) which lead us into temptation.) What is the result as stated in **verse 21**?

_____

_____

_____

_____

_____

KINGDOM ENCOUNTER
TEMPTATION & TRIALS – SESSION #5

IV BIBLE STUDY   continued
   B HOW DO PEOPLE GET CAUGHT IN TEMPTATION?   Continued

SUMMARIZE THE MAIN THOUGHTS FROM THE VERSES IN SECTION B

   C AVOIDING, RESISTING & OVERCOMING TEMPTATION
   1 What can a believer do to avoid temptation? Describe your findings in the following verses:
   • **Matthew 26:41**

_____
_____
_____

   • **James 4:7-8**

_____
_____
_____

   • **Proverbs 4:14-15**

_____
_____
_____

   2 The LORD shows us many ways to withstand temptation. Explain your findings:
   • **Ephesians 6:11-18**

_____
_____
_____

   • **Psalms 119:11**

_____
_____
_____

   • **Proverbs 2:10-12a**

_____
_____
_____

   • **Proverbs 3:5-6**

_____
_____
_____

IV BIBLE STUDY   continued
C   AVOIDING, RESISTING & OVERCOMING TEMPTATION

SUMMARIZE THE MAIN THOUGHTS FROM THE VERSES IN SECTION C

D   NATURE OF TRIALS – and where do they come from?

> **TRIALS** (testing and challenging circumstances) come from various sources. They are allowed by God, and many times given by HIM for the purpose to strengthen and grow us; and to test our faith in HIM. There are also **TRIALS** that occur due to the choices we make; and because He gave us **"FREE WILL"** He will not always intervene to save us from ourselves. God did not make us to be robots, and therefore allows us to use our **"free will"** to make deadly choices. The good news is that HE is with us every step in our life, always lovingly waiting for us to voluntarily return to HIM.

1   What was the purpose or reason for these trials, and who or what caused them, as described in the following verses:
   - **Jeremiah 9:7**

_____

_____

   - **Exodus 20:20**

_____

_____

_____

   - **Jeremiah 17:10**

_____

_____

2   How do trials affect believers spiritually, emotionally, or physically?
   - Explain the **SPIRITUAL** aspects of the trial in **Hebrews 11:17-19**

_____

_____

_____

_____

IV **BIBLE STUDY**   continued
   D **NATURE OF TRIALS – and where do they come from?**   continued
   2   How do trials affect believers spiritually, emotionally, or physically?   ...continued
   - Describe the **EMOTIONS** Job must have felt and explain his response to this test allowed by God. Read **Job 1:13-21**.

_____

_____

_____

   - The **PHYSICAL** affliction that Paul suffered in **2 Corinthians 12:7-10**, had what effect on him? What was the lesson to be learned?

_____

_____

_____

SUMMARIZE THE MAIN THOUGHTS FROM THE VERSES IN SECTION D

   E **TRIALS AFFECT BELIEVERS – painful, insufferable, seemingly without purpose – BUT GOD!**
   1   Ask the Holy Spirit to give you wisdom for your own life as you discover the purpose behind these trials:
   - **Isaiah 48:10-11** Describe what God did and why?

_____

_____

_____

   2   **1 Peter 4:12-16** Describes an in-depth explanation of God's reasoning behind difficult trials:
   - **Verse 12** Imagine that you are in the middle of a particularly difficult trial, what is God saying here that could apply to you?

_____

_____

_____

   - **Verse 13** What is being said about trials you might face?

_____

_____

_____

_____

KINGDOM ENCOUNTER
TEMPTATION & TRIALS – SESSION #5

IV BIBLE STUDY   continued
   E TRIALS AFFECT BELIEVERS – painful, insufferable, seemingly without purpose – BUT GOD!
   2 **1 Peter 4:12-16** Describes an in-depth explanation of God's reasoning behind difficult trials:
   - **Verse 14** What are the effects of trials in relationship to Christ, Holy Spirit, God our Father, and the benefit for you?

_____
_____
_____

   - **Verse 15** What is the "involvement" that should be avoided in respect to other people's affairs?

_____
_____
_____

   - **Verse 16** What can we expect as a Christian?

_____
_____
_____

   3 **Hebrews 12:5-11** Explain why we are chastened by the LORD?

_____
_____
_____

   4 **Romans: 5:3-5** What does tribulation produce in us?

_____
_____

SUMMARIZE THE MAIN THOUGHTS FROM THE VERSES IN SECTION E

   F **HOW TO RESPOND TO TRIALS**
   1 The following verses describe appropriate responses to similar trials and challenges we face in our life.
   - **James 1:2-4** What do these verses say about trials?

_____
_____
_____
_____

KINGDOM ENCOUNTER
TEMPTATION & TRIALS – SESSION #5

IV **BIBLE STUDY**   continued
   F **HOW TO RESPOND TO TRIALS**   continued
      1 The following verses describe appropriate responses to similar trials and challenges we face in our life.   ...continued

- **2 Corinthians 12:9-10**   When Paul faced this trial, what was his attitude toward God; and how might this help us face our own trials?

_____

_____

      2 Explain how **Romans 8:28 and vs. 38-39** provides assurance for ultimate victory?

_____

_____

      3 Describe how applying this example from the life of Jesus given in **Hebrews 12:1-3** will help you face temptation and trials.

_____

_____

_____

SUMMARIZE THE MAIN THOUGHTS FROM THE VERSES IN SECTION F

   G   **OVERCOMING SOUL ISSUES THAT BLOCK VICTORY OVER TEMPTATION & TRIALS**

We are made in God's image. **GOD is:** *The Father, the Son, and the Holy Spirit.* **WE ARE:** *Body, Soul and Spirit*; and ***at our spiritual center is our HEART***. The **HEART** *"denotes a person's center for both physical and emotional-intellectual-moral activities*; sometimes it is used figuratively for any inaccessible thing." (Baker's Evangelical Dictionary of Biblical Theology – Heart)

The **SOUL is:** ***The Mind, Will and Emotions***. The **MIND** is the control center to the brain (mind over matter); *what the **MIND** allows into the brain determines our mental, physical, and emotional response and reaction to all life circumstances*. The **MIND**, directing the brain, affects the physical functions of the **BODY** and may work with or be at odds with the **SPIRIT** of man.

All SOUL (mind, will, emotions) issues affect the condition of our HEART.
Proverbs 23:7 "As a man thinks in his heart so is he. "

IV BIBLE STUDY   continued

G   OVERCOMING SOUL ISSUES THAT BLOCK VICTORY OVER TEMPTATION & TRIALS   ...continued

> God has given us **"Free Will"**, and thus we can use our **MIND** to choose our direction in life, and the resulting consequences – both good and bad – are the *FRUIT of those choices*. When we accept Jesus Christ as our Lord and Savior, by faith our **SPIRIT, BODY, and SOUL** (Mind, Will & Emotions) begin to align with our God-given destiny and purpose; enabling us to live a **KINGDOM LIFESTYLE**.

1   Under the 3 topics listed below, explain what the Holy Spirit is revealing to you regarding the contrast between **THE WORLD** and **GOD'S KINGDOM**:

- **FREE WILL** Describe the choice God gives to His people in **Deuteronomy 30:19**.

_____

_____

- **MIND** When it comes to our mental ability, what are believers able to obtain that is not available to the "natural man" according to **1 Corinthians 2:1-16**?

_____

_____

- **FRUIT** Contrast the "fruit" available to Believers in **Galatians 5:22-23** with the "fruit" available to the world?

_____

_____

_____

2   When our **SOUL & SPIRIT** are in conflict it is difficult to overcome temptation and trials. Read **Romans 7:15** and explain what gets in the way of our victory.

_____

_____

> One major **SOUL ISSUE** that affects our ability to have victory over **TEMPTATION & TRIALS** is a **"STRONGHOLD"** erected in the **MIND**.
>
> The **MIND** creates a filter, developed from birth, through which we receive, store, and distribute information. All experiences, and our thoughts about them, become memories and create our filter system. **This filter system *allows or prohibits* new information from flowing into your mind; and adds its perspective on what is allowed to stay there. This filter is what we call our **MINDSET**. (A **MINDSET**, *working contrary to God's plan for your life, creates* STRONGHOLDS) The good news is that God says we can change our **MINDSET** (*breaking down unhealthy strongholds*) to work for us instead of against.
>
> This is why God says in **Romans 12:2** *"And do not be conformed to this world, but be transformed by the renewing of your mind, that you may prove what is that good and acceptable and perfect will of God."*

KINGDOM ENCOUNTER
TEMPTATION & TRIALS – SESSION #5

IV BIBLE STUDY   continued

  G   OVERCOMING SOUL ISSUES THAT BLOCK VICTORY OVER TEMPTATION & TRIALS. ...continued

   3   Practically applying the following verses by the power of the Holy Spirit will show you how to breakdown strongholds, redirect your thinking and reactions and change your **MINDSET** into alignment with the **KINGDOM OF GOD**.

   - **2 Corinthians 10:3-5** How do you pull down strongholds (mindsets)? Describe your findings?

   _____

   _____

   - **Philippians 4:8** What should we be thinking about? How would that make a difference in changing our **MINDSET**?

   _____

   _____

   - **Proverbs 16:3** What practice will establish correct thinking?

   _____

   _____

   - **Philippians 4:6-7** Describe God's plan for achieving a proper mindset.

   _____

   _____

   - **Proverbs 4:20-23** Refer to the NEW LIVING TRANSLATION for real clarity. What is God specifically telling his children to do in relationship to the HEART?

   _____

   _____

ACKNOWLEDGEMENT: A resource used for this section is **SWITCH ON YOUR BRAIN** by Dr. Carolyn Leaf. "*'Switch On Your Brain' teaches you the science and Scripture behind the amazing God-given power we have within our minds*" – Joyce Meyer

---

SUMMARIZE THE MAIN THOUGHTS FROM THE VERSES IN SECTION G

_____

_____

_____

_____

_____

KINGDOM ENCOUNTER
TEMPTATION & TRIALS – SESSION #5

V SUMMARY & APPLICATION

SUMMARY - Write out the verse that is most meaningful to you from each section in this session.

A NATURE OF TEMPTATION

B HOW DO PEOPLE GET CAUGHT IN TEMPTATION

C AVOIDING, RESISTING & OVERCOMING TEMPTATION

D NATURE OF TRIALS

E TRIALS AFFECT BELIEVERS – painful, insufferable, seemingly without purpose – BUT GOD!

F HOW TO RESPOND TO TRIALS

G HOW TO OVERCOME SOUL ISSUES

APPLICATION - think about these questions, write your thoughts if you wish to do so, or save them for class discussion.

1   Based on what you learned do you feel better equipped to handle temptation. Explain.

_____

_____

2   What did you learn that might help when you are tested?

_____

_____

_____

3   In what ways does knowing more about SOUL ISSUES give you new insight into how to deal with temptation and trials?

_____

_____

_____

NOTES

KINGDOM ENCOUNTER

SPIRITUAL WARFARE
SESSION #6

SPIRITUAL WARFARE is the battle for our soul, this side of heaven.
This is a strategic battle waged against all of mankind by Satan and his demonic forces.

Satan's battle plan is to "kill, steal, and destroy" our life by any means necessary;
and specially to convince us that we are unworthy to accept the gift of eternal life
in the **KINGDOM OF GOD**.

In this session you will learn tactics and strategy to
withstand the enemy of your soul and wage successful **SPIRITUAL WARFARE**.

KINGDOM ENCOUNTER
Our Group Prayer Sheet

MEMBERS:

	Name	Email	Cell Phone
1			
2			
3			
4			

Praises & Prayer Requests

"As for me, far be it from me that I should sin against the Lord by failing to pray for you." 1 Samuel 12:23

Date	Praises/Prayer Requests	Date	Answers

KINGDOM ENCOUNTER
SPIRITUAL WARFARE – SESSION #6

I INTRODUCTION

SPIRITUAL WARFARE is the battle for our soul, this side of heaven. This is a strategic battle waged against all of mankind by Satan and his demonic forces. His plan is to keep us out of the **KINGDOM OF GOD**, living a defeated life, and settling for the **KINGDOM OF DARKNESS**. Jesus Christ by his death on the cross and resurrection has defeated the devil. By His sacrifice, in the power of the Holy Spirit, as Born-Again Believers, we have the keys to His Kingdom and the authority to accept eternal life if we choose it.

Our Father in Heaven has given us **FREE WILL** to choose **SALVATION** through **JESUS CHRIST**; or stay in darkness. ***God allows us to choose our lifestyle and eternal dwelling place***. Even if we are Born Again Believers, **FREE WILL** means ***we can choose to walk away from Jesus Christ***. However, Jesus promises believers that we cannot be stolen from His Father by saying, ***"and no one is able to snatch them out of My Father's hand." (John 10:29b)*** Satan's battle plan is to "kill, steal, and destroy" our life by any means necessary; and specially to convince us that we are unworthy to accept the gift of eternal life in the **KINGDOM OF GOD**. In this session you will learn tactics and strategy to withstand the enemy of your soul and wage successful **SPIRITUAL WARFARE.**

II GOD SPEAKS TO YOU THROUGH HIS WORD: write out the memory verse.

A Memory Verse: (Use the New Living Translation) Colossians 2:8

| |
| |
| |
| |
| |

B Analysis Questions

1 Knowing the enemy doesn't use obvious methods of warfare, what do you think is a good battle plan?

_____

_____

2 What are some of the empty philosophies and high-sounding nonsense that might draw you away from Jesus Christ?

_____

_____

_____

3 Who might try to capture your mind so you would listen to the world rather than Jesus Christ?

_____

_____

_____

_____

III DEFINE: SPIRITUL WARFARE (Using Biblical resources)

_____

_____

_____

_____

IV BIBLE STUDY

A WHAT IS SPIRITUAL WARFARE

The **Kingdom of God** versus the **Kingdom of Darkness** – the battle for our souls!

Spiritual Warfare requires that we **RESIST THE DEVIL** and **STAND FIRM** by **FAITH in the VICTORY** already won by **Jesus Christ** by his death on the cross and resurrection.

1 What does **1 Peter 5:9** suggest is our battle plan with the devil?

_____

_____

2 In **Ephesians 2:1-3** Paul speaks about how he and his listeners were once lost in sin. Describe what they overcame, and explain what causes people to be called "sons of disobedience" (as described in **verse 3**)

_____

_____

3 **Ephesians 6:11-12** states a great deal about our enemy and his territory. The first thing we are told to do is put on the whole armor of God so we can stand against the wiles of the devil. Then there is a list of characteristics and description of who and what we face. Describe what you know, or what the Holy Spirit is revealing to you about our enemy:

- What are the **"Wiles of the devil"**?

_____

_____

- What are **Principalities?**

_____

_____

- What kind of **Powers**?

_____

_____

- Who or what are the **"Rulers of the darkness of this age"**?

_____

_____

KINGDOM ENCOUNTER
SPIRITUAL WARFARE – SESSION #6

IV **BIBLE STUDY continued**

  A **WHAT IS SPIRITUAL WARFARE   continued**

    3 **Ephesians 6:11-12** ......our enemy: continued

      • Who are the **"spiritual hosts of wickedness"** residing in heavenly places?

_____

_____

SUMMARIZE THE MAIN THOUGHTS FROM THE VERSES IN SECTION A

  B **THE ENEMY'S PLAN TO DEFEAT MANKIND**

    1 Deception is a key tactic of the devil. Describe the situation and what took place in the following verses:

      • **Genesis 2:16-17** What specifically did God tell Adam?

_____

_____

      • **Genesis 3:1-3** How did the serpent's question put doubt in the mind of Eve?

_____

_____

      • **Genesis 3:2-3** What did Eve specifically tell the serpent?   What did she add to her answer that was different than what God told Adam? Why?

_____

_____

      • **Genesis 3:4-5** What did the serpent say to convince Eve that it was a good idea to eat the fruit of the tree?

_____

_____

      • **Genesis 3:6-7** By her actions, what did she believe to be true? As a result, what happened to Adam and Eve at that moment?

_____

_____

_____

KINGDOM ENCOUNTER
SPIRITUAL WARFARE – SESSION #6

IV **BIBLE STUDY continued**
  B **THE ENEMY'S PLAN TO DEFEAT MANKIND   continued**

    2   In each verse explain Satan's tactics against humanity, who he is targeting, and what he hopes to achieve:

- **Mark 4:15**

_____
_____

- **Job 2:3-7**

_____
_____
_____

- **2 Corinthians 4:3-4**

_____
_____
_____

    3   When Adam and Eve sinned by falling for the devil's deception, they lost their position of authority over the kingdoms of the earth. Immediately Satan was given the power and authority – but then came JESUS.

- **Luke 4:5-7**   Explain what the devil hoped to accomplish?

_____
_____

- **Luke 4:8**   What was Jesus' response?   Did Satan have the authority to give Jesus all the Kingdoms of the world?   (Notice that Jesus did not get into a discussion with the Devil)

_____
_____
_____

SUMMARIZE THE MAIN THOUGHTS FROM THE VERSES IN SECTION B

KINGDOM ENCOUNTER
SPIRITUAL WARFARE – SESSION #6

IV   BIBLE STUDY continued
C   WARFARE WITH THE WORLD

As a believer you are no longer of this world, your home is in the Kingdom of God. Yet the enemy of your soul will stop at nothing to entice you to remain in bondage, yielding to the things of this world, instead of enjoying freedom in the Lord Jesus Christ. **"Therefore, if the Son makes you free, you shall be free indeed" John 8:36**

1   What does the world value that are in opposition to God according to **1 John 2:16**?

_____

2   What kind of adverse consequences will the love of the world produce in our life according to the following verses?

   • **James 4:4**

_____

   • **1 John 2:15**

_____

_____

   • **Timothy 4:3-4**

_____

_____

SUMMARIZE THE MAIN THOUGHTS FROM THE VERSES IN SECTION C

D   WARFARE WITH THE FLESH

Those who allow their mind to be filled with sensual pleasures and desires apart from God develop a **"Fleshy or Carnal" Mindset**. They are easily drawn off from living a Kingdom of God lifestyle. To gratify the desires of their flesh they leave themselves open to the schemes of the devil. The following verses describe Spiritual Warfare with the flesh.

1   Read **Romans 8:5-7** and describe the difference between living for the Spirit or living a carnal, fleshy lifestyle. What is the outcome?

_____

_____

_____

KINGDOM ENCOUNTER
SPIRITUAL WARFARE – SESSION #6

IV **BIBLE STUDY continued**
  D **WARFARE WITH THE FLESH**   continued

   2   Read **Galatians 5:19-21** and summarize the works of the flesh.

_____
_____
_____
_____

   3   Describe what must be done to change the fleshly mindset according to **Ephesians 4:22-24**.

_____
_____
_____
_____

   4   Read **Romans 6:10-14** and describe how to win the spiritual war against the flesh.

_____
_____
_____
_____

SUMMARIZE THE MAIN THOUGHTS FROM THE VERSES IN SECTION D

  E **WARFARE WITH SATAN**

Satan and his army have a battle plan. He has lost the ultimate war, but nevertheless until Jesus comes back, he's up to the same tactics. Ask the Holy Spirit to reveal the countermeasures you must use to effectively resist your adversary.

   1   Explain what the Holy Spirit is revealing to you about Satan's warfare tactics as described in the following verses?

      • **1 Chronicles 21:1-3, 7** What tactic(s) did Satan use against David? Why did it work?

_____
_____
_____

      • **1 Peter 5:8** How could you get caught unaware?

_____
_____
_____
_____

KINGDOM ENCOUNTER
SPIRITUAL WARFARE – SESSION #6

IV **BIBLE STUDY continued**

    E   **WARFARE WITH SATAN**   **continued**

        1   Explain what the Holy Spirit is revealing to you about Satan's warfare tactics as described in the following verses?   **continued**

            • **2 Corinthians 11:13-15** How can we be fooled?

_____

_____

            • **1 Corinthians 7:5** Why is this one of Satan's most successful tactics?

_____

            • **Luke 22:31** What did Satan want to do to Peter?

_____

_____

            • **Ephesians 4:26-27** What should we be careful not to do?

_____

_____

SUMMARIZE THE MAIN THOUGHTS FROM THE VERSES IN SECTION E

    F   **THE WEAPONS OF OUR WARFARE**

        1   What weapon did Jesus use in **Matthew 4, verses 4, 7, 10** – State the three powerful words and why was it effective.

_____

_____

        2   According to **Philippians 4:6-7** how does prayer prepare you for spiritual warfare?

_____

_____

        3   Explain how the plan outlined in **James 4:7-10** is used to overcome the devil.

_____

_____

_____

F   THE WEAPONS OF OUR WARFARE   continued

4   In **Ephesians 6:10-18** Our enemy is described and the weapons we use. The weapons are outlined below; explain what they are and why you need them – what part of your body is protected?

- **Verse 14   Belt of Truth**

_____

_____

- **Verse 14   Breastplate of Righteousness**

_____

_____

- Verse 15   **Your feet are shod with what and why?**

_____

_____

- **Verse 16   Shield of Faith – what will this piece of armor do for you?**

_____

_____

- **Verse 17   Helmet of salvation**

_____

_____

- **Verse 17   Sword of the Spirit (Holy Spirit) – Is this an offensive or defensive weapon? Explain your answer.**

_____

_____

- **Verse 18   Once one is clothed in the Armor of God, what must the SPIRITUAL WARRIOR do always? Explain your answer.**

_____

_____

_____

_____

SUMMARIZE THE MAIN THOUGHTS FROM THE VERSES IN SECTION F

KINGDOM ENCOUNTER
SPIRITUAL WARFARE – SESSION #6

IV BIBLE STUDY continued

   G SPIRITUAL WARFARE – HOW WE OVERCOME

     1 According to **Romans 12:2** what are key strategies for you to know? How will this help you?

_____

_____

_____

_____

     2 Read **1 John 4:4-6** and explain why a believer can have boldness and confidence against the enemy?

_____

_____

_____

_____

_____

     3 What does **Luke 10:17-19** explain about the authority Jesus gave to the believer?

_____

_____

_____

_____

     4 Read **Colossians 2:13-15** and explain how we are assured of victory in Christ.

_____

_____

_____

_____

     5 Explain how we know that we won the Spiritual War as stated in **Romans 8:37-39**.

_____

_____

_____

_____

SUMMARIZE THE MAIN THOUGHTS FROM THE VERSES IN SECTION G

KINGDOM ENCOUNTER
SPIRITUAL WARFARE – SESSION #6

V SUMMARY & APPLICATION

SUMMARY - Write out the verse that is most meaningful to you from each section in this study.

A	WHAT IS SPIRITUAL WARFARE

B	THE ENEMY'S PLAN TO DEFEAT MANKIND

C	WARFARE WITH THE WORLD

D	WARFARE WITH THE FLESH

E	WARFARE WITH SATAN

F	THE WEAPONS OF OUR WARFARE

G	SPIRITUAL WARFARE – HOW WE OVERCOME

APPLICATION – think about these questions, write your thoughts if you wish to do so, or save them for class discussion.

1   What do you personally do to resist the devil and his schemes against you?

_____

_____

2   In this session what did you find most helpful to understand about the war for your soul?

_____

_____

_____

3   Which piece(s) of the "armor of God" do you rely on most?   Why?

_____

_____

_____

_____

NOTES

KINGDOM ENCOUNTER
SPIRITUAL WARFARE – SESSION #6

NOTES

KINGDOM ENCOUNTER

OBEDIENCE
SESSION #7

We enter the Kingdom of God by our faithful obedience to our Lord and Savior Jesus Christ. The Bible promises spiritual blessings as we abide in Him and are then able to live a Kingdom Lifestyle on earth as it is in Heaven.

In this session you will learn that OBEDIENCE is the path to a personal relationship with our Lord Jesus Christ. Through the power of the Holy Spirit the believer is shown how to be obedient.

KINGDOM ENCOUNTER
Our Group Prayer Sheet

MEMBERS:

	Name	Email	Cell Phone
1			
2			
3			
4			

Praises & Prayer Requests

"As for me, far be it from me that I should sin against the Lord by failing to pray for you." 1 Samuel 12:23

Date	Praises/Prayer Requests	Date	Answers

KINGDOM ENCOUNTER
OBEDIENCE – SESSION #7

I   INTRODUCTION:

We enter the Kingdom of God by our faithful obedience to our Lord and Savior Jesus Christ. The Bible promises spiritual blessings as we abide in Him and are then able to live a Kingdom Lifestyle. To abide in Christ means willing obedience to the Word of God. Man in his sinful nature does not submit to God's authority on his own, thus it is through the power of the Holy Spirit that the believer is shown how to be obedient. The Holy Spirit encourages the believer to forsake the ways of this world and follow Christ in word and deed.

Although obeying God's commandments may at times seem difficult the rewards are worth the effort. Obedience is the path to a personal relationship with our Lord Jesus Christ and to the open door of His abundant love and grace in our lives.

II   GOD SPEAKS TO YOU THROUGHT HIS WORD: write out the memory verse.

A   Memory Verse: **Deuteronomy 6:4-6**

B   Analysis Questions

1   How does the statement in verse 4 answer the question about the nature of God?

2   How are we to love God?

3   Where is God in relationship to all else in our lives?

4   Of all the other things we hold in our heart, which words should be first?

KINGDOM ENCOUNTER
OBEDIENCE – SESSION #7

III   DEFINE: OBEDIENCE (Using Biblical resources)

_____

_____

_____

IV   BIBLE STUDY

A   NATURE OF OBEDIENCE

1   God created mankind to establish His Kingdom on earth, which required obedience to His commandments. What was the significance of **Genesis 2:16-17**?

_____

_____

2   Abraham was called the Father of Faith because He obeyed God. He first obeyed when God told him to leave Ur of the Chaldees and go to a new land. His second act of obedience is found in **Genesis 22:1-19**. What does **Verse 5** state that indicates Abraham's faith in God?

_____

_____

3   In the Old Testament God instilled the value of obedience into His people Israel. Look for the application in our lives today. _**In the following verses explain the value of obedience and the consequences (if applicable, for disobedience):**_

- **Exodus 19:5-6**   What did God promise to Israel if they obey Him?

_____

_____

- **Deuteronomy 6:1-2**   How are these commandments applicable to us today?

_____

- **Deuteronomy 6:4-6**   What did God command of Israel and us?

_____

- **Deuteronomy 6:7-9**   What did God expect Israel to do with His Words? How do we apply this today?

_____

_____

- **Deuteronomy 11:26-28**   Explain the consequences of obedience and disobedience.

_____

_____

_____

KINGDOM ENCOUNTER
OBEDIENCE – SESSION #7

IV   BIBLE STUDY continued
A   NATURE OF OBEDIENCE   continued

3   In the Old Testament God instilled the value of obedience into His people Israel. Look for the application in our lives today. In the following verses explain the value of obedience and the consequences (if applicable, for disobedience):   ...continued

- **1 Samuel 13:13-14** - Explain how Saul's example of disobedience might be applicable for us and particularly in leadership roles.

_____

_____

4   Jesus describes the nature of obedience as giving us 2 choices when faced with a decision to follow God or not. Each choice lays the foundation for our lifetime. Describe the difference between the two foundations in **Luke 6:46-49.**

_____

_____

SUMMARIZE THE MAIN THOUGHTS FROM THE VERSES IN SECTION A

B   BLESSINGS OF OBEDIENCE
Our Kingdom Lifestyle is blessed when we are obedient to God's commandments. God first blessed His people, Israel, and as born-again believers those blessings follow our obedience to Him today. ***Describe the commandment and the blessing from each of the following verses:***

- **Deuteronomy 5:32-33**

_____

_____

- **Deuteronomy 28:2-8** These blessings were given to God's people Israel and also apply to anyone who obeys the voice of the Lord.

_____

_____

- **Psalm 119:97-101**

_____

_____

IV BIBLE STUDY continued

B BLESSINGS OF OBEDIENCE continued

Our Kingdom Lifestyle is blessed when we are obedient to God's commandments. God first blessed His people, Israel, and as born-again believers those blessings follow our obedience to Him today. Describe the commandment and the blessing from each of the following verses: **...continued**

- **Proverbs 1:33**

_____

_____

_____

- **Jeremiah 7:23**

_____

_____

_____

- **1 John 2:5**

_____

_____

_____

SUMMARIZE THE MAIN THOUGHTS FROM THE VERSES IN SECTION B

C OBEDIENCE OF CHRIST

Jesus Christ was fully man and fully God. He was sent to be the sacrificial lamb to pay the price for our sins by His death on the cross and by His resurrection gave us the gift of eternal life in the Kingdom of Heaven. Observe what **OBEDIENCE** means through these examples from the life of Jesus Christ.

1   According to **John 6:38** what is the reason that Jesus came from heaven?

_____

_____

2   In **Romans 5:19-21** we see the consequences of Adam's disobedience. Describe the result of Christ's obedience?

_____

_____

_____

_____

KINGDOM ENCOUNTER
OBEDIENCE – SESSION #7

IV BIBLE STUDY continued

  C OBEDIENCE OF CHRIST   continued

Observe what **OBEDIENCE** means through these examples from the life of Jesus Christ. ...continued

1 **Philippians 2:8** Describe what was required of Jesus as a man in the flesh.

_____

_____

2 **John 8:28-29** – What event is Jesus describing to His disciples? What was His purpose in explaining the details in this manner?

_____

_____

3 Read **John 10:17-18** and describe the relationship Jesus has with his Father, and the power that remained in Him as God in the flesh.

_____

_____

4 **Luke 22:42** – why do you think Jesus prayed this prayer to His Father?

_____

_____

5 In **John 15:9-10** – what can we expect if we obey Jesus?

_____

_____

6 Read **Hebrews 5:7-9**. Describe when and how Jesus learned to be obedient. How did that become an example for us?

_____

_____

_____

SUMMARIZE THE MAIN THOUGHTS FROM THE VERSES IN SECTION C

KINGDOM ENCOUNTER
OBEDIENCE – SESSION #7

IV BIBLE STUDY continued
D THE COMMITMENT OF OBEDIENCE

When we accept Jesus Christ as our Lord and Savior we agree to follow and obey Him; and to turn from our past sinful ways. That means obedient commitment to doing life His way instead of following the world.

1   What does the Bible say in **1 Samuel 15:22** about obedience?

_____

_____

2   In **Psalm 37:5** what are the action steps and the results?

_____

_____

3   What are the choices regarding obedience as explained in **Romans 6:16**?

_____

_____

_____

4   Read **Ephesians 4:22-24** and explain the process of becoming obedient to God?

_____

_____

_____

5   According to **Psalm 40:8** what should characterize a believer's obedience?

_____

_____

6   How does **Colossians 3:17** explain that a believer should respond in all his endeavors?

_____

_____

7   According to **Romans 12:1-2** how do we become obedient to God and then know His Will for our lives?

_____

_____

8   Read **Joshua 24:14-15** – describe the choices Joshua outlined for God's people and the commitment he and his household made. How does that apply to us today?

_____

_____

9   Commitment is all about obeying God's commandments. What are the two greatest commandments described in **Matthew 22:37-40**?

_____

_____

_____

KINGDOM ENCOUNTER
OBEDIENCE – SESSION #7

IV   BIBLE STUDY continued

D   THE COMMITMENT OF OBEDIENCE   continued

SUMMARIZE THE MAIN THOUGHTS FROM THE VERSES IN SECTION D

E   THE DISCIPLINE OF OBEDIENCE

It is a walk of faith that requires perseverance in the power of the Holy Spirit to develop the **DISCIPLINE OF OBEDIENCE**. Once we develop that lifestyle the rewards are life altering! Learn how to live it out in the following verses:

- **Colossians 3:1-2** Where do we find what we are looking for?

_____

_____

- **Hebrews 12:1-3** What discipline must we have and what is our goal?

_____

_____

- **Galatians 2:20** What is our sacrifice and what can we expect in return?

_____

_____

- **Acts 4:18-20** How did Peter and John walk out their commitment to obey God?

_____

_____

- Read **2 Corinthians 6:16-18**. In **Verses 17-18** What does God require of us? What are the benefits?

_____

_____

- **John 14:21** What is the discipline of obedience stated here?

_____

_____

- **James 1:22** In what way do we deceive ourselves?

_____

_____

KINGDOM ENCOUNTER
OBEDIENCE – SESSION #7

IV **BIBLE STUDY continued**
E **THE DISCIPLINE OF OBEDIENCE**

SUMMARIZE THE MAIN THOUGHTS FROM THE VERSES IN SECTION E

F **SPIRITUAL GROWTH THROUGH OBEDIENCE**

Your commitment to live in obedience to God the Father, His son, Jesus Christ in the power of the Holy Spirit results in exponential spiritual growth. Observe what your pathway to success looks like in this section.

1 **Deuteronomy 12:28** What is God's promise for our obedience?

_____

2 **2 Corinthians 5:7** Describe the contrast between a Believer's journey through life and the way of the world.

_____

3 Read **2 Corinthians 10:4-6.** How does **OBEDIENCE** figure into the battle we wage in this life? Why is your spiritual growth crucial to your success?

_____

4 **Philippians 2:12-15** Describe the Spiritual walk of obedience in the following verses:
   - **Verse 12** How should we react to our own salvation?

_____

   - **Verse 13** How does God work in us?

_____

   - **Verse 14** How should we go about our calling in life?

_____

   - **Verse 15** When we are obedient, what can we expect in life and from the world?

_____

5 **1 Peter 3:15** How do we prepare ourselves to react to the world?

_____

IV BIBLE STUDY continued

    F SPIRITUAL GROWTH THROUGH OBEDIENCE   continued

SUMMARIZE THE MAIN THOUGHTS FROM THE VERSES IN SECTION F

V SUMMARY & APPLICATION

    SUMMARY - Write out the verse that is most meaningful to you from each section in this study.

A NATURE OF OBEDIENCE

B BLESSINGS OF OBEDIENCE

C OBEDIENCE OF CHRIST

D THE COMMITMENT OF OBEDIENCE

E THE DISCIPLINE OF OBEDIENCE

F SPIRITUAL GROWTH THROUGH OBEDIENCE

APPLICATION – think about these questions, write your thoughts if you wish to do so, or save them for class discussion.

1   What has the Holy Spirit shown you regarding your own level of obedience as a follower of Jesus Christ?

_____

_____

_____

_____

_____

V   SUMMARY & APPICATION continued

APPLICATION – think about these questions, write your thoughts if you wish to do so, or save them for class discussion.   ...continued

2   Are there any changes you think would make your life more in alignment with God's will for you?

_____
_____
_____
_____
_____

3   Do you look at **OBEDIENCE** any differently than before this lesson? If so, how?

_____
_____
_____
_____
_____

NOTES

_____
_____
_____
_____
_____
_____
_____
_____
_____
_____
_____
_____
_____
_____
_____
_____
_____
_____
_____

KINGDOM ENCOUNTER
OBEDIENCE – SESSION #7

NOTES

KINGDOM ENCOUNTER

PRAYER
SESSION #8

Prayer is your opportunity for a KINGDOM ENCOUNTER,
bringing heaven to earth every time you speak to God.

As this session unfolds you will see principles throughout scripture
that provide insight into receiving what you ask for in prayer.
While it may seem a mystery when you ask and don't receive
what you ask for, scripture provides clarity
that will change how you look at your prayer life.

KINGDOM ENCOUNTER
Our Group Prayer Sheet

MEMBERS:

	Name	Email	Cell Phone
1			
2			
3			
4			

Praises & Prayer Requests

"As for me, far be it from me that I should sin against the Lord by failing to pray for you." 1 Samuel 12:23

Date	Praises/Prayer Requests	Date	Answers

KINGDOM ENCOUNTER
PRAYER – SESSION #8

I   INTRODUCTION

Prayer is your opportunity for a KINGDOM ENCOUNTER, bringing heaven to earth every time you speak to God. Through His son, Jesus Christ, you have a direct line of communication and the power of the Holy Spirit to intercede on your behalf.

As this session unfolds you will see principles throughout scripture that provide insight into receiving what you ask for in prayer. While it may seem a mystery when you ask and don't receive what you ask for, scripture provides clarity that will change how you look at your prayer life.

II   GOD SPEAKS TO YOU THROUGH HIS WORD: write out the memory verse.

    A   Memory Verse: 1 John 5:14-15

    B   Analysis Questions

       1   How can we be assured that God is listening to us?

       2   If we know that He hears us what can we expect from Him?

       3   Do you place a time frame for His response to your prayers?

       4   Is there anything you wish you knew before you prayed?

KINGDOM ENCOUNTER
PRAYER – SESSION #8

III DEFINE: PRAYER (Using Biblical resources)

_____

_____

_____

_____

IV BIBLE STUDY continued

A HOW PRAYER BEGAN

> When God created man, He walked with him in the garden of Eden, He talked with Adam as a father to his son. There was no separation between God and Adam; he was connected to the source of all things. And Eve also benefited in the same manner. There was no need for mankind to **PRAY** and ask God to supply anything. They had it all.
>
> When Satan deceived Eve, and Adam sinned, they both were cast out of the Garden. They lived under the curse that God pronounced on the ground, on themselves and their children. **PRAYER** was needed to restore their broken relationship with God. However, there is no record of the word **PRAYER** in scripture for hundreds of years after the fall of man. Mankind was aware of God, some even honored Him as the creator and provider. Eventually mankind began to "Call on God" or "Walk with God," but the term "prayer" is not found in the Bible before the flood. After the flood, when mankind began seeking answers to life's challenge and petitioning God with their requests these actions were clearly called **PRAYER.**

1   The first Biblical record of what many theologians consider the beginning of **PRAYER** is found in **Genesis 4:26** – explain your findings.

_____

_____

2   As we are looking at how **PRAYER** began, the next term that is highlighted in scripture is the reference to those that "walked with God." According to **Genesis 5:22-24** who was Enoch? How many years did he "walk with God?" And what was most special about his life?

_____

_____

3   In the years before the flood, as it is today, God looked at how mankind lived before Him. What we would call a **PRAYER LIFE** could be likened to whether someone "called on the name of the Lord" or how they "walked with him".   One such man, Noah, the great, great grandson of Enoch, is described in **Genesis 6:8-9, 13-14, and 22** – who was he, why was he favored and what was he called to do?

_____

_____

_____

_____

KINGDOM ENCOUNTER
PRAYER – SESSION #8

IV BIBLE STUDY continued
A HOW PRAYER BEGAN   continued

The flood marked a new beginning for mankind. 8 people walked off the Ark along with the birds and animals that were saved with them; and together they would repopulate the earth. God blessed Noah and his family and told them to be fruitful and multiply. (See **Genesis 9:1**-7 for details)

1   In the following verses describe what Noah did and how God reacted. Explain how these verses are a turning point for mankind. That people would realize God cared for them by His actions here, and that they could expect Him to regard their needs and hear their prayers.

- **Genesis 8:20-21**

_____

_____

_____

- **Genesis 9:8-11, and 13**

_____

_____

_____

SUMMARIZE THE MAIN THOUGHTS FROM THE VERSES IN SECTION A

B WHY WE PRAY

PRAYER that God hears occurs when we ask God to help us solve our life situations according to **His Will.** If you personalize the **"Lord's Prayer"** into the way you and I speak, you might say, "My Father, who is in heaven, Holy is Your name. Your Kingdom, come into my life; Your Will be done in my life as it is in Heaven. Give me this day…..**the answer to my prayer**." The Holy Spirit activates God's Will in our lives as we pray. His Will is that we would encounter His Kingdom on earth every time we pray. Throughout God's Word we see that prayers are answered when we pray that **His Will is done** in whatever situation we raise up to Him.

1   The reason that we should pray is given as the first commandment of the ten (10) he gave to mankind. Read **Deuteronomy 6:5** and explain why it is important to your prayer life.

_____

_____

_____

_____

KINGDOM ENCOUNTER
PRAYER – SESSION #8

IV **BIBLE STUDY continued**
   B **WHY WE PRAY**   **continued**

     2   How does prayer keep us from sin according to **1 Samuel 12:23**?

_____

_____

     3   What does God say he wants from us when we pray to Him as found in
       2 Chronicles 7:14? What then will He do for us?

_____

_____

     4   What disasters could be avoided if someone prayed according to **Ezekiel 22:30**?

_____

_____

     5   Why is our faith an important part of our prayer life as described in **Hebrews 11:6**?

_____

_____

     6   According to **Mark 14:38** how do we conduct ourselves in prayer, and what are the
       benefits?

_____

_____

     7   Why do you think that praying as described in **James 5:16** is so effective?

_____

_____

     8   What does **Luke 21:36** say is the ultimate benefit to be watchful and pray?

_____

_____

SUMMARIZE THE MAIN THOUGHTS FROM THE VERSES IN SECTION B

KINGDOM ENCOUNTER
PRAYER – SESSION #8

IV   BIBLE STUDY continued

   C   **WHAT TO DO – your prayer attitude**

      There are enumerable ways to pray, to develop your own prayer attitude. Keep in mind that God loves you, knows your thoughts, and the intent of your heart. He especially delights in hearing your voice and wants to answer your prayers. The following verses illustrate some of the ways one can pray and help you to develop your way of speaking to God.

- **Psalms 27:7-8**   What is the Psalmist asking of God?

_____

_____

- **Psalms 62:8**   What is the believer told to do?

_____

_____

_____

- **Romans 8:26**   Who do we rely on if we don't know how to pray?

_____

_____

- **Hebrews 4:14-16**   When we feel weak where do we find strength and the confidence to pray?

_____

_____

- **1 Thessalonians 5:17**   What is the command to follow? Is this something you do now? If not, how do you think you could bring this action into your life?

_____

_____

_____

- **Philippians 4:6**   How should you present your request to God?

_____

_____

_____

- **1 Timothy 2:8**   What does God desire from us?

_____

_____

SUMMARIZE THE MAIN THOUGHTS FROM THE VERSES IN SECTION C

KINGDOM ENCOUNTER
PRAYER – SESSION #8

IV   BIBLE STUDY continued
D   HOW JESUS TAUGHT PRAYER

When Jesus' disciples asked him how to pray, he gave them this model to follow. We call it the Lord's Prayer. But more than that it is a pattern of principles that God wants to hear from us when we petition him with our requests. *WITHOUT GETTING TOO RELIGIOUS IN THE APPLICATION OF THESE PRINCIPLES* – understand that God does not require that you use every piece of this pattern for him to listen to you. God looks first at the intent of your heart. This exercise will provide ideas of elements you may want to bring into your own prayer life. It's especially useful if you "journal" or like to write out prayer requests. Not on the fly when you find yourself in circumstances that you need the help of the Holy Spirit for an immediate pressing situation. The simple prayer: "God help me!" or "I need you now!" also work just fine because He knows your thoughts and your circumstances.

Using **Matthew 6:9-13**, write out each verse of the Lord's Prayer. Then using the additional scripture write out the explanation of the verse in the "Lord's Prayer". The similar elements in the additional verse will expand your understanding and give you some new ideas to express yourself in prayer. The first one is done for you, using an example from my thought process. Ask the Holy Spirit what He wants you to learn as you write out this section.

1   [This one is done for you] Write our **Matthew 6:9 (Use Psalm 150:1-2 for your explanation)**

VERSE 9: "In this manner, therefore, pray: Our Father in heaven, Hallowed be Your name."

Using Psalm 150:1-2 "Praise the LORD! Praise God in His sanctuary; Praise Him in His mighty firmament! [2] Praise Him for His mighty acts; Praise Him according to His excellent greatness!"

Explanation: "**Our Father in heaven**" - God desires recognition for who He is and even where He resides – when I pray, I acknowledge his position, or his location as being in Heaven, His sanctuary, he's God of the Universe, etc. "**Hallowed be Your name**" - I make "praising Him" part of my prayers, because His name is holy and must be honored, along with his mighty acts, and His excellent greatness.

2   Write out **Matthew 6:10 (Use Mark 14:36 for your explanation)**

_____

_____

3   Write out **Matthew 6:11** (Use **Philippians 4:19** for your explanation)

_____

_____

_____

_____

KINGDOM ENCOUNTER
PRAYER – SESSION #8

IV   BIBLE STUDY continued
    D   HOW JESUS TAUGHT PRAYER   continued
        4   Write out **Matthew 6:12** (Use **Mark 11:25-26** for your explanation)

_____

_____

_____

_____

        5   Write out **Matthew 6:13** (Use **1 Corinthians 10:13** for your explanation)

_____

_____

_____

_____

_____

SUMMARIZE THE MAIN THOUGHTS FROM THE VERSES IN SECTION D

   E   WHY SOME PRAYERS GO UNANSWERED
God makes it clear in the Bible why he will not answer some prayers; why in fact He doesn't even listen. This section will focus on those reasons. In the next section we will focus on answered prayers.
- **James 1:6-7**   What must one possess to get his prayers answered?

_____

_____

- **James 4:3**   Explain why certain prayers are not answered.

_____

_____

- **Job 35:12-13**   Describe when and why God does not answer.

_____

_____

- **Isaiah 59:2**   What separates one from God, and what is His reaction?

_____

_____

_____

KINGDOM ENCOUNTER
PRAYER – SESSION #8

IV   BIBLE STUDY continued
    E   WHY SOME PRAYERS GO UNANSWERED   continued

- **Proverbs 1:25-28** Describe this situation and how it could be prevented.

_____

_____

- **Zechariah 7:11-13** What was the Lord's response to these people?

_____

_____

- **Proverbs 21:13** What must we be careful to do?

_____

_____

- **Jeremiah 11:11-14** Do you see any similarity with what is going on in today's society? What is the warning we should heed?

_____

_____

SUMMARIZE THE MAIN THOUGHTS FROM THE VERSES IN SECTION E

F   HOW ARE PRAYERS ANSWERED

God delights to answer our prayers and give us good gifts. Sometimes answers come quickly, and sometimes they are delayed. And of course, sometimes the answer is "NO". The Holy Spirit will guide you in knowing when to persist and not give up. ***As Ps Jurgen Matthesius (Awaken Church Lead Pastor) says – PUSH – pray until something happens!***

1   Read **Luke 11:9-10** How will this advice help you?

_____

_____

2   Paraphrase **1 John 5:14-15** in your own words and explain how you can know that your prayers will be answered.

_____

_____

_____

IV BIBLE STUDY continued
  F HOW ARE PRAYERS ANSWERED   continued
    3   **Isaiah 65:24** Has this ever happened to you? Explain.

_____

_____

    4   **Hebrews 11:6** What must a believer do to get his prayers answered?

_____

    5   What lessons can **Proverbs 3:5-6** provide?

_____

_____

    6   We all have desires in our heart that we wish God would fulfill. Jesus provides helpful
        insight into how to ask and be assured of success. Read **John 15:7** and explain your answer.

_____

_____

    7   When sickness is related to sin in one's life, what type of prayer will heal that person
        according to **James 5:14-15**?

_____

_____

    8   Jesus talked about agreement in prayer in **Matthew 18:19-20**. Explain what impact 2 or
        more praying together can have in receiving what they ask for.

_____

_____

    9   What should we do when we don't receive an answer to our prayer right away? If we don't
        like the answer, how should we regard it? How is the Holy Spirit speaking to you as you
        read the following verses? Explain in each verse how it might apply in your own
        experience; when you seek an answer that is delayed or not what you wanted.
        • **Isaiah 55:8**

_____

_____

        • **2 Peter 3:8**

_____

_____

IV   BIBLE STUDY continued
    F   HOW ARE PRAYERS ANSWERED   continued

    Explain in each verse how it might apply in your own experience – when you seek an answer that is delayed or not what you wanted.   ...**continued from page 9.**

       • **Romans 8:28**

_____

_____

_____

       • **Ephesians 3:20**

_____

_____

SUMMARIZE THE MAIN THOUGHTS FROM THE VERSES IN SECTION F
.

V   SUMMARY - Write out the verse that is most meaningful to you from each section in this study.

A   HOW PRAYER BEGAN

B   WHY WE PRAY

C   WHAT TO DO – your prayer attitude

D   HOW JESUS TAUGHT PRAYER

E   WHY SOME PRAYERS GO UNANSWERED

F   HOW ARE PRAYERS ANSWERED

V   APPLICATION - Think about these questions, write your thoughts if you wish to do so, or save them for class discussion.

1   What did you learn that will be most helpful for your prayer life?

_____
_____
_____
_____
_____
_____

2   Did you learn anything about yourself through this session?

_____
_____
_____
_____
_____
_____

3   In what ways does God speak to you when you pray?   (Example: Audible, in dreams or visions, or some other way)

_____
_____
_____
_____
_____
_____
_____

NOTES

_____
_____
_____
_____
_____
_____
_____
_____
_____
_____
_____
_____

NOTES

_____
_____
_____
_____
_____
_____
_____
_____
_____
_____
_____
_____
_____
_____
_____
_____
_____
_____
_____
_____
_____
_____
_____
_____
_____
_____
_____
_____
_____
_____
_____
_____
_____
_____

KINGDOM ENCOUNTER
PRAYER – SESSION #8

NOTES

_____
_____
_____
_____
_____
_____
_____
_____
_____
_____
_____
_____
_____
_____
_____
_____
_____
_____
_____
_____
_____
_____
_____
_____
_____
_____
_____
_____
_____
_____
_____
_____
_____
_____
_____
_____

KINGDOM ENCOUNTER

FELLOWSHIP
SESSION #9

Fellowship is a close personal relationship believers have with Jesus Christ,
by the power of the Holy Spirit, along with a deep commitment to each other.

In this session you will delve into all aspects of Biblical FELLOWSHIP.
Look for the practical application in your life and in your own fellowship groups,
and within the church at large. The Kingdom of God that Jesus established on earth
is designed to be the fellowship of His saints.

KINGDOM ENCOUNTER
Our Group Prayer Sheet

MEMBERS:

	Name	Email	Cell Phone
1			
2			
3			
4			

Praises & Prayer Requests

"As for me, far be it from me that I should sin against the Lord by failing to pray for you." 1 Samuel 12:23

Date	Praises/Prayer Requests	Date	Answers

KINGDOM ENCOUNTER
FELLOWSHIP – SESSION #9

I   INTRODUCTION

Fellowship is a close personal relationship believers have with Jesus Christ, by the power of the Holy Spirit, along with a deep commitment to each other. *"For by one Spirit we were all baptized into one body – whether Jews or Greeks, whether slaves or free--and have all been made to drink into one Spirit."* **1 Corinthians 12:12-13**.

In this session you will delve into all aspects of **Biblical FELLOWSHIP**. Look for the practical application in your life and in your own fellowship groups, and within the church at large. The **Kingdom of God** that Jesus established on earth is designed to be the fellowship of His saints.

II   GOD SPEAKS TO YOU THROUGH HIS WORD: write out the memory verse.

   A   Memory Verse: Philippians 2:1-2 (Use the New Living Translation)

   B   Analysis Questions

   1   What is Apostle Paul hoping these believers would take to heart from **verse 1**?

   2   What is probably going on with these believers as Paul admonishes them to correct their attitude?

   3   What is the practical application of this verse in your own fellowship groups?

   4   Is the Holy Spirit showing you anything from these verses that you know is just for your benefit?

III **DEFINE: FELLOWSHIP** (Using Biblical Resources)

_____

_____

_____

_____

IV BIBLE STUDY

A WHAT IS FELLOWSHIP

It is more than a superficial relationship. **FELLOWSHIP** is a deep personal and spiritual unity among individuals and people groups that surpasses other relationships. Biblical fellowship is empowered by the Holy Spirit and is a deep commitment one to another.

1 In the beginning God's plan as part of creation was that mankind should not be alone. Describe how God's plan brought mankind into relationship with one another.

- **Genesis 2:18**

_____

_____

- **Genesis 2:20**

_____

_____

- **Genesis 2:21-25** Give your thoughts on how the first human relationship was the foundation for the deep unity that becomes what we call **FELLOWSHIP**.

_____

_____

_____

2 In this Old Testament example, how did God unify this group of people, and what was the result? Consider what this would mean if an entire nation lived in this kind of **FELLOWSHIP** with each other. Read **2 Chronicles 30:12** (The whole chapter is a wonderful blueprint for how one bold king of Judah changed the course of his nation, Israel)

_____

_____

_____

3 As stated in **1 Corinthians 1:9**, how is a person called into "fellowship"?

_____

_____

_____

KINGDOM ENCOUNTER
FELLOWSHIP – SESSION #9

IV   BIBLE STUDY continued

A   WHAT IS FELLOWSHIP   continued

4   The Apostle John is describing what the disciples had personally experienced as they followed Jesus. What was the outcome he hoped to achieve for those he was witnessing to?   Read **1 John 1:1-4.**

_____

_____

SUMMARIZE THE MAIN THOUGHTS FROM THE VERSES IN SECTION A

B   UNITED IN FELLOWSHIP

Biblical FELLOWSHIP is described by the Greek word, Koinonia, which is a deep sense of spiritual unity – communion with the Lord, by the Holy Spirit, and between believers.

1   In these verses in **John 17:20-23** explain what Jesus accomplished in the disciples and what it would mean for the world.

- **Verse 20**   Jesus refers to the future mandate that His disciples would have – what was Jesus praying for and what would be the result?

_____

_____

- **Verse 21**   What did Jesus want for His disciples? What did He want the world to believe?

_____

_____

- **Verse 22**   What did Jesus give them that His Father had given Him, what did it do for them?

_____

_____

- **Verse 23**   With Jesus in his disciples and God the Father in Jesus – how does that bring perfection? What did Jesus pray that the world would know?

_____

_____

KINGDOM ENCOUNTER
FELLOWSHIP – SESSION #9

IV   BIBLE STUDY continued

    B   UNITED IN FELLOWSHIP   continued

        2   What does **Acts 2:42-47** describe as important aspects to **FELLOWSHIP**? What are the similarities to present day "fellowship" groups?

_____

_____

        3   What must a believer do to be united in fellowship as described in **1 John 4:20-21**?

_____

_____

        4   In the following verses explain what it means to be UNITED IN FELLOWSHIP – the comparison here uses our physical body as a symbol of the body of Christ which is His Church. Read **1 Corinthians 12:14-25**.

            • **Verse 14   FELLOWSHIP** requires more than one participant, what is the point here?

_____

_____

            • **Verses 15-17**   Although a rather peculiar discussion, what is the main point?

_____

_____

_____

            • **Verses 18-19**   What is God's perspective on the "Body"?

_____

_____

_____

            • **Verses 20-22**   In **verse 22** what is God's position on the members of the "Body"?

_____

_____

_____

            • **Verses 23-24a**   How do we look at the "Body"? (**Stop at the end of 24a**)

_____

_____

_____

            • **Verse 24b - 25**   As God looks at the "Body" (of Christ) how does he see it differently than we do? What does that say about us having unity in fellowship with one another?

_____

_____

_____

_____

_____

IV   BIBLE STUDY continued

    B   UNITED IN FELLOWSHIP   continued

SUMMARIZE THE MAIN THOUGHTS FROM THE VERSES IN SECTION B

    C   PURPOSE OF FELLOWSHIP

We understand that Fellowship is our relationship with each other in Christ by the Holy Spirit. The purpose of fellowship is to activate the gifts of the Holy Spirit in the body of Christ – His Church.

1   What are the main points relating to the purpose of Fellowship in **Romans 12:4-5**?

_____

_____

2   Apostle Paul, in **1 Thessalonians 2:10-12** outlines how his team set an example for this fellowship of believers, "as a father does his own children." In **verse 12**, what is the ultimate purpose?

_____

_____

3   What is the purpose and benefits of Fellowship as outlined in **Hebrews 10:24-25**?

_____

_____

4   The following verses express the importance and purpose God places on being in **FELLOWSHIP.** Explain your findings.
   - **Proverbs 27:17**

_____

_____

   - **Matthew 18:20**

_____

_____

_____

_____

IV   BIBLE STUDY continued
C   PURPOSE OF FELLOWSHIIP   continued

4   The following verses express the importance and purpose God places on being in FELLOWSHIP. Explain your findings.   ...continued

- **1 Corinthians 1:9**

_____
_____
_____

- **Corinthians 8:13-15**

_____
_____

- **Ephesians 4:3**

_____
_____
_____

- **Philippians 2:3-4**

_____
_____
_____

- **1 John 4:20-21**

_____
_____
_____

SUMMARIZE THE MAIN THOUGHTS FROM THE VERSES IN SECTION C

D   WHAT HINDERS FELLOWSHIP

1   The simplest way to hinder and destroy our fellowship with one another is the devil's scheme to cause division, doubt, loss of focus and any of the common afflictions that cause mankind to fall into sin. As well as what is in this fallen world. Here are a few reminders – explain your findings.

- **Genesis 3:1**

_____
_____
_____

IV   BIBLE STUDY continued

D   WHAT HINDERS FELLOWSHIP   continued

1   The simplest way to hinder and destroy our fellowship with one another is the devil's scheme to cause division, doubt, loss of focus and any of the common afflictions that cause mankind to fall into sin. As well as what is in this fallen world. Here are a few reminders – explain your findings.   ...continued

- **1 Peter 5:8**

_____

_____

- **1 John 2:16**

_____

_____

2   What principle was Jesus trying to get across to His disciples so as not to hinder their fellowship? Read **Luke 22:24-27.**

_____

_____

3   What did Paul observe in **1 Corinthians 1:10** that was a problem in their fellowship; and what corrective action did he ask them to take?

_____

_____

4   Here are some hindrances to Fellowship. Explain the hindrance and the remedy in the following verses:

- **Matthew 7:1-5**

_____

_____

- **James 2:8-9**

_____

_____

- **1 John 1:8**

_____

_____

- **1 John 1:9** This is the remedy - Explain why not taking this action would be a hindrance.

_____

_____

- **1 John 3:4**

_____

_____

KINGDOM ENCOUNTER
FELLOWSHIP – SESSION #9

IV   BIBLE STUDY continued
    D   WHAT HINDERS FELLOWSHIP   **continued**
        4   Here are some hindrances to Fellowship. Explain the hindrance and the remedy in the following verses: ...continued
               • **2 Corinthians 6:14**

_____

_____

SUMMARIZE THE MAIN THOUGHTS FROM THE VERSES IN SECTION D

    E   KINGDOM FELLOWSHIIP

This is God's design for Fellowship –Koinonia – deep commitment one to another in Christ by the power of His Holy Spirit. As we remember, Jesus came to bring the Kingdom of God to earth, and hence establish **KINGDOM FELLOWSHIP** among believers.

        1   In the following verses in **Acts 2** observe what happened at Pentecost which led to the establishment of this fellowship model. Notice how this pattern is often replicated in fellowship groups today.
               • **Acts 2:3-6** What happened that caught the attention of the multitude so that they came together, and who were they?

_____

_____

_____

               • **Acts 2:7-12** Why did they marvel, and what were the reasons they were so amazed?

_____

_____

               • Read Peter's sermon, **Acts 2:14-36**. Referring to verse 36, what was Peter's summary of this message?

_____

_____

_____

_____

KINGDOM ENCOUNTER
FELLOWSHIP – SESSION #9

IV **BIBLE STUDY continued**

  E   **KINGDOM FELLOWSHIP**   continued

    1   Referring to **Acts 2** and the establishment of this fellowship model.   ...continued

        • How did this mixed multitude react, and what did Peter explain to them as found in **Acts 2:37-40?**

_____

_____

_____

    2   From the following verses, describe how this pattern of Koinonia – **KINGDOM FELLOWSHIP** was established.

        • **Acts 2:41-42** How were these believers united in fellowship?

_____

_____

        • **Acts 2:43-45** Explain the key points about their fellowship?

_____

_____

        • **Acts 2:46-47** Describe their daily activities, their attitude toward God and each other and how other people treated them. Why do you think the Lord added to their numbers daily?

_____

_____

    3   After Pentecost, there was a multitude of new believers from diverse backgrounds that established a fellowship. Describe your findings from **Ephesians 3:9**? Check other translations for clarity.

_____

_____

_____

SUMMARIZE THE MAIN THOUGHTS FROM THE VERSES IN SECTION E

KINGDOM ENCOUNTER
FELLOWSHIP – SESSION #9

V   SUMMARY & APPLICATION
SUMMARY – Write out the verse that is most meaningful to you from each section in this study.

A   WHAT IS FELLOWSHIP
B   UNITED IN FELLOWSHIP
C   PURPOSE OF FELLOWSHIP
D   WHAT HINDERS FELLOWSHIP
E   KINGDOM FELLOWSHIP

APPLICATION – think about these questions, write your thoughts if you wish to do so, or save them for class discussion.

1   In what ways did this session cause you to think differently about the importance of fellowship?

_____

_____

_____

_____

_____

2   Why is it important that the Holy Spirit be in the midst of our fellowship with one another?

_____

_____

_____

_____

_____

3   What do you think is the main purpose of fellowship?

_____

_____

_____

_____

_____

_____

KINGDOM ENCOUNTER
FELLOWSHIP – SESSION #9

NOTES

KINGDOM ENCOUNTER

WITNESSSING
SESSION #10

Witnessing to the goodness of God
is the privilege we share with all believers.

This session will show you how to use
your God-given assignment along with the testimony of your life
as a practical application of the gospel.
Witnessing in this manner is what draws people
into the Kingdom of God.

KINGDOM ENCOUNTER
Our Group Prayer Sheet

MEMBERS:

	Name	Email	Cell Phone
1			
2			
3			
4			

Praises & Prayer Requests

"As for me, far be it from me that I should sin against the Lord by failing to pray for you." 1 Samuel 12:23

Date	Praises/Prayer Requests	Date	Answers

KINGDOM ENCOUNTER
WITNESSING – SESSION #10

I INTRODUCTION

Witnessing to the goodness of God is the privilege we share with all believers. It goes beyond the moment of our salvation, when we accepted Jesus Christ as our Lord and Savior, and welcomed Holy Spirit as our guide. Our witness is one Gospel in two parts; the "Gospel of the Kingdom of God" Christ preached and the "Gospel of Salvation" that secures our inheritance as a son or daughter of God our Heavenly Father.

Our God-given assignment is to use the testimony of our life as a practical application of the Gospel. Each of us has a unique destiny and purpose only we can fulfill. Daily we work out our salvation, increasing our faith by the power of the Holy Spirit, and building our testimony as we persevere to live a Kingdom Lifestyle. Witnessing in this manner is what draws people into the Kingdom of God.

II GOD SPEAKS TO YOU THROUGH HIS WORD: write out the memory verse.

A Memory Verse: Acts 1:8

B Analysis Questions:

1 Where does the power come from to be a witness?

2 What did Jesus want shared to the end of the earth?

3 Why do you suppose Jesus told them to start in Jerusalem, all Judea and then Samaria, before going to the rest of the world?

4 Any other thoughts about this verse?

KINGDOM ENCOUNTER
WITNESSING – SESSION #10

III **DEFINE: WITNESSING** (Using Biblical Resources)

_____

_____

_____

IV **BIBLE STUDY**

  A   **WITNESS – THE GOSPEL**

The **WITNESS** we share with the world is the multifaceted gospel message. Jesus Christ taught and demonstrated to His disciples the reason God His Father sent him to earth. He came to redeem and reconcile the world back to God, to establish His Kingdom on earth. At His baptism, the Holy Spirit came upon Jesus, God the Father confirmed Him as His Son, and at that point the Kingdom was with Jesus Christ. After His death and resurrection, the gospel message included Salvation as the only way to enter the Kingdom of God.

  1   What was the central theme to the gospel message in these verses?

  • **Matthew 4:17**

_____

  • **Matthew 10:7**

_____

  • **Mark 1:14-15**

_____

_____

  2   What message is to be preached as a **"WITNESS"** to all the nations? Read **Matthew 24:14.**

_____

The "GOSPEL" (Greek: good news) Jesus preached is the message of the Kingdom of God, and that He was the only way to God the Father. (Remember that He had not yet gone to the cross) Following His death and resurrection the disciples, new believers, and the Apostle Paul preached the "Gospel of Salvation" which is the only way to enter the Kingdom of God - by faith in Jesus Christ. As Apostle Paul stated in **Ephesians 1:13, i**n Him you also trusted, after you heard the word of truth, the gospel of your salvation; in whom also, having believed, you were sealed with the Holy Spirit of promise.

  3   Although "repentance" is the first step, there are other equally important elements to understand and include as part of our WITNESS when we share the GOSPEL. In this section discover many of those elements as you answer the questions.

  • **Isaiah 61:1** (use NIV) Jesus read this verse in the temple – why this verse?

_____

_____

KINGDOM ENCOUNTER
WITNESSING – SESSION #10

IV   BIBLE STUDY continued

    A   WITNESS – THE GOSPEL

        3   Besides "repentance" what are some of the other elements we can include in our WITNESS when we share the GOSPEL of Jesus Christ?   Continued

- **John 14:6**   What did Jesus say was the only way to the Father?

- **Hebrews 11:6**   Why is FAITH so important?

- **James 2:18**   Explain the relationship between FAITH and WORKS?

- **Matthew 7:21**   What is the importance of doing God's WILL?

- **Matthew 18:3**   Why is being "childlike" important?

- **Ephesians 1:7**   How does HIS GRACE play a part in our redemption?

SUMMARIZE THE MAIN THOUGHTS FROM THE VERSES IN SECTION A

    B   WITNESS – KINGDOM PARABLES

> Jesus preached that He came to bring the KINGDOM OF GOD to earth. That mankind would first have to repent; and then be restored before he could live a Kingdom Lifestyle on earth and look forward to the eternal Kingdom. In this section, using examples that people of that time could relate to, He tells what the Kingdom is like. Be thinking how these parables could be useful to share when you witness to others.

KINGDOM ENCOUNTER
WITNESSING – SESSION #10

IV   BIBLE STUDY continued

B   WITNESS – KINGDOM PARABLES

1   Were parables understandable to everyone? Why not? Read **Luke 8:10** and explain.

_____

_____

_____

2   There are 7 Kingdom Parables found in **Matthew 13**. As you read them, allow the Holy Spirit to show you a practical application for sharing about Jesus and living the Kingdom Lifestyle in this present age.

- **Matthew 13:1-9 Parable of the Sower**. In the first of the Kingdom Parables, in what way does this remind you of what it's like to share about Jesus with your friends.

_____

_____

- **Matthew 13:24-30 Parable of the Wheat and Tares**. Then read the explanation in **verses 36-43** how does this help you understand the kingdom on earth and what Jesus will do to establish the final kingdom? **Verses 41-43** are particularly helpful.

_____

_____

- **Matthew 13:31-32   Parable of the Mustard Seed**. If you think of the mustard seed (Kingdom) as an idea that is both received and then shared, how does that relate to our WITNESS?

_____

_____

_____

- **Matthew 13:33 Parable of the Leaven.** How does this explain the expansion of the Kingdom?

_____

_____

- **Matthew 13:44 Parable of the Hidden Treasure.** How should one look at the Kingdom?

_____

_____

_____

_____

KINGDOM ENCOUNTER
WITNESSING – SESSION #10

IV   **BIBLE STUDY continued**
    B   **WITNESS – KINGDOM PARABLES**
       The 7 Kingdom Parables   continued

- **Matthew 13:45-46   Parable of the Pearl of Great Price.** Ask yourself, how much value do I put on the Kingdom?

_____

_____

- **Matthew 13:47-50   Parable of the Dragnet.** This story of what fisherman do with their catch has what application in our lives?

_____

_____

3   After Jesus had shared these parables about the Kingdom of Heaven, what did he want His disciples to understand? How can we apply that same understanding when we witness to others? Read **Matthew 13:51-52.**

_____

_____

SUMMARIZE THE MAIN THOUGHTS FROM THE VERSES IN SECTION B

C   **WITNESS – HOW TO ENTER**

We have the ultimate choice whether to enter the Kingdom of Heaven or not. It is a free gift but requires submission to God as our Father, Jesus as our Lord and Savior and the Holy Spirit as our guide – a triune God. The steps we have taken is what we share as our WITNESS to others, helping them to decide whether to make that choice.

1   **REPENTANCE** – what does it mean to repent? We understand that it is to turn away from sin. Discover in this section what it means to God that we repent of sin as the first step toward entering His Kingdom.

- **2 Chronicles 7:14** What comes after repentance (turning from wicked ways)?

_____

_____

_____

_____

IV   BIBLE STUDY continued

    C   WITNESS – HOW TO ENTER

        1   **REPENTANCE**   continued

- **2 Corinthians 7:10** Contrast godly sorrow and the sorrow of the world.

_____

_____

- **Luke 15:7** Why is there more joy over one sinner?

_____

_____

- **Romans 2:4** What leads to repentance?

_____

_____

- **Timothy 2:24-26** How should one witness to others? What part does repentance play in the process?

_____

_____

- **Peter 3:9** What value does the Lord place on repentance?

_____

_____

        2   **FORGIVENESS** – this step involves asking God to forgive us the sins we have committed as well as forgiving others. Unforgiveness blocks our way to entering the Kingdom of Heaven. Explain the most important aspect of "forgiveness" in each of the following verses.

- **Matthew 6:15**

_____

_____

- **Luke 6:37**

_____

_____

- **Acts 8:22**

_____

_____

- **Acts 26:17-18**

_____

_____

_____

- **1 John 1:9**

_____

_____

_____

IV   **BIBLE STUDY** continued

   C   **WITNESS – HOW TO ENTER**   continued

     3   **REDEMPTION/RECONCILATION – SALVATION - BY FAITH** - Our own righteousness will not redeem us. *"For Christ is the end of the law for righteousness to everyone who believes." Romans 10:4*

- **Romans 1:16-17**   What is the power of God to salvation?

_____

_____

- **Romans 10:6-9**   How is one saved?

_____

_____

_____

- **2 Corinthians 5:18-19**   Explain reconciliation through Jesus Christ.

_____

_____

- **Ephesians 1:7**   How are we redeemed?

_____

- **1 Peter 1:18-19**   What were we redeemed from?

_____

_____

_____

- **Colossians 2:13**   What made us alive with Him?

_____

- **James 5:15**   What does the prayer of faith do?

_____

     4   **COMMITMENT – pledge to follow Jesus.** Explain your findings in the following verses.

- **Psalm 37:5**

_____

- **Psalm 31:5**

_____

_____

IV   BIBLE STUDY continued
   C   WITNESS – HOW TO ENTER   continued
      4   COMMITMENT   continued
        • Proverbs 16:3

_____

_____

_____

        • Matthew 10:38

_____

_____

        • John 10:27

_____

_____

        • John 12:26

_____

_____

SUMMARIZE THE MAIN THOUGHTS FROM THE VERSES IN SECTION C

D   WITNESS – TESTIMONY OF PAUL – Damascus Road Conversion
   1   As you read how Paul witnessed the Gospel of Salvation to Felix and King Agrippa, notice the points of his testimony. These elements are similar in the testimony of every believer— their life before Jesus, the turning point, the moment they were saved, how their life has changed and where they are now.
      • **Acts 24:25** Why do you think Felix sent Paul away? How is this like your own experience when you try to talk to someone about Jesus?

_____

_____

HIS PAST – before Jesus
      • **Acts 26:9-11** What did Paul do to Christians? Why did he share this part?

_____

_____

_____

KINGDOM ENCOUNTER
WITNESSING – SESSION #10

IV   BIBLE STUDY continued

  D   WITNESS – TESTIMONY OF PAUL – Damascus Road Conversion   continued

<u>TURNING POINT</u>

- **Acts 26:12-14**   What got Paul's attention, so he knew he had to change course?

_____

_____

_____

<u>SALVATION</u>

- **Acts 26:15-17**   What do you think went through Paul's mind? The fact that he called him "Lord", is this an indication of what Paul would be willing to do?

_____

_____

_____

_____

<u>ASSIGNMENT FROM JESUS</u>

- **Acts 26:17-18** What are the main points of Paul's assignment?

_____

_____

_____

_____

<u>LIVING FOR JESUS</u>

- **Acts 26:19-20**   How would you use this message, "repent, turn to God, and do works befitting repentance" as practical advice for how we are to live?

_____

_____

_____

- **Acts 26:22-23**   How does Paul say he witnesses for Christ?

_____

_____

_____

SUMMARIZE THE MAIN THOUGHTS FROM THE VERSES IN SECTION D

KINGDOM ENCOUNTER
WITNESSING – SESSION #10

IV   BIBLE STUDY continued
     E   WITNESS – DEVELOPING YOUR TESTIMONY

Sharing what God has done in your life is the most powerful way to attract people to want to know Jesus Christ. You are unique in creation, with a special assignment only you can fulfill. Nobody else has experienced life in the same way you have, and you may be the only one that certain people will listen to. Even if you have experienced an awful childhood, difficult adult life, with addiction, abuse, and disasters left and right. God promises to turn everything to good, for those who love Him and are called according to His purposes. People, living just like you were, are waiting to hear what God has done for you

In this section you will write out a short version of your testimony, choosing the most important points, which you can use when you only have a few minutes to share with someone. This testimony will help you organize your thoughts so you can talk at length in other situations. To prepare, refer to Apostle Paul's Damascus Road conversion in the previous section; and answer the following questions:

1   What was your life like before you knew God?

_____

_____

_____

2   Turning Point – How bad did your life get before you realized you had to do something different? Even if you don't think it was terrible, there still was a "turning point" for you – describe it.

_____

_____

_____

3   Did you try some other way to improve your life, before you considered Jesus Christ?

_____

_____

4   What got you to consider Jesus?

_____

_____

5   When and How did you accept Jesus Christ as your Lord and Savior?

_____

_____

_____

IV   BIBLE STUDY continued

E   WITNESS – DEVELOPING YOUR TESTIMONY   continued

6   **How is your life now?** This is the most important part of your testimony. Not a time to be "religious" – remember it's about your "relationship" with God – you are His child, and He loves you. Share the main victories, what you have overcome, when he has been there for you in tough situations, any miracles in your life. Sharing your favorite verse and how that guides your life can be really encouraging. Ask the Holy Spirit what He would have you share. Pick the most important moments to highlight.

_____
_____
_____
_____
_____
_____
_____
_____
_____
_____
_____
_____
_____
_____

Write your testimony using the points you outlined above: (Remember this is a short version)

_____
_____
_____
_____
_____
_____
_____
_____
_____
_____
_____
_____
_____
_____
_____
_____

KINGDOM ENCOUNTER
WITNESSING – SESSION #10

V   SUMMARY & APPLICATION

SUMMARY – Write out the verse that is most meaningful to you from each section in this study

A WITNESS – THE GOSPEL
B WITNESS – KINGDOM PARABLES
C WITNESS – HOW TO ENTER
D WITNESS – TESTIMONY OF PAUL – his Damascus Road Conversion
E WITNESS – DEVELOPING YOUR TESTIMONY – write a favorite verse that you might use as part of your testimony.

APPLICATION – think about these questions, write your thoughts if you wish to do so, or save them for class discussion.

1   Did you learn something about **WITNESSING** that you didn't know before?

_____

_____

_____

2   In the **KINDGOM PARABLES**, which one do you find most helpful?

_____

_____

_____

3   In the section on **HOW TO ENTER**, is there anything you discovered that you might share when you speak to a non-believer?

_____

_____

_____

_____

_____

KINGDOM ENCOUNTER
WITNESSING – SESSION #10

NOTES

KINGDOM ENCOUNTER

MINISTRY – HEALING & DELIVERANCE
SESSION #11

The Bible is God's manual for how to live successfully in His Kingdom.
Ministry is the active expression of this pattern of life
whereby we fulfill the Great Commandment.

This session will help you grasp the POWER and AUTHORITY
you have been given to minister to God's people, by His HOLY SPIRIT,
in the same manner Jesus taught His disciples to HEAL & DELIVER.

KINGDOM ENCOUNTER
Our Group Prayer Sheet

MEMBERS:

	Name	Email	Cell Phone
1			
2			
3			
4			

Praises & Prayer Requests

"As for me, far be it from me that I should sin against the Lord by failing to pray for you." 1 Samuel 12:23

Date	Praises/Prayer Requests	Date	Answers

KINGDOM ENCOUNTER
MINISTRY – HEALING & DELIVERANCE – SESSION #11

I INTRODUCTION

The Bible is God's manual for how to live successfully in His Kingdom. Ministry is the active expression of this pattern of life whereby we fulfill the Great Commandment: "You shall love the Lord your God with all your heart, with all your soul, and with all your mind" and "You shall love your neighbor as yourself" (**Matthew 22:37,39**)

While there are "differences of ministries, diversities of activities, and the manifestation of the Spirit is given to each one for the profit of all: "...one and the same Spirit works all these things, distributing to each as He wills" (Reference: **1 Corinthians 12:4-11**). This session will help you grasp the POWER and AUTHORITY you have been given to minister to God's people, by His HOLY SPIRIT, in the same manner Jesus taught His disciples to HEAL & DELIVER.

II GOD SPEAKS TO YOU THROUGH HIS WORD: write out the memory verse.

A MEMORY VERSE: Matthew 10:7-8

B Analysis Questions

1 Why were the disciples told to preach the message that "the Kingdom of heaven was at hand?"

2 If Jesus commands believers to do something on His behalf, why do we doubt that we can do it? Doesn't a commandment come with authority?

3 What is meant by "Freely you have received, freely give?"

KINGDOM ENCOUNTER
MINISTRY – HEALING & DELIVERANCE – SESSION #11

III DEFINE: MINISTRY (Using Biblical Resources)

_____
_____
_____
_____

IV BIBLE STUDY
A   EMPOWERED FOR MINISTRY

ALL MINISTRY is empowered by the person we call the **HOLY SPIRIT; the third person of the Godhead**. Our Lord Jesus only began his ministry after He was water baptized and then received the Holy Spirit. *We are empowered to minister when we receive the baptism of the HOLY SPIRIT.* This section will lay the foundation for ministry as modeled by Jesus Christ.

1   In **Mark 1:14-15** Jesus lays the groundwork for His ministry in this message – explain the main points.

_____
_____
_____
_____

2   Preparation for Ministry – Read **Luke 4:1-15**
- **Verses 1-2** Why was he led into the wilderness?

_____
_____
_____
_____

- **Verses 12-13** What was Jesus' reply to the devil?

_____
_____

- **Verses 14-15** What empowered Jesus for ministry? How does the process affect anyone going into ministry?

_____
_____
_____

3   What did Jesus say was His assignment, and describe how He was prepared for ministry according to **Luke 4:18**?

_____
_____
_____
_____

IV   BIBLE STUDY continued

  A   EMPOWERED FOR MINISTRY continued

  4   Jesus prayed His Father would prepare His disciples, and all believers that would come afterwards for their ministry assignment. **In these verses describe the preparation of those that would be sent out into the world.**

- **John 17:10-11**

_____

_____

- **John 17:21** What did Jesus ask His Father to do for believers?

_____

_____

- **John 17:15-18**

_____

_____

  5   In **Matthew 28:18-20** what authority do believers have, and what are they told to do?

_____

_____

_____

SUMMARIZE THE MAIN THOUGHTS FROM THE VERSES FROM SECTION A

  B   AUTHORITY & POWER

  1   In these verses from **Matthew 10**, Jesus prepares his disciples to follow in His footsteps and minister healing and deliverance to hurting people.

- **Verse 1** How were the disciples prepared to minister?

_____

_____

- **Verses 5-8** Where were the disciples to go and what were they to say and do?

_____

_____

_____

KINGDOM ENCOUNTER
MINISTRY – HEALING & DELIVERANCE – SESSION #11

V   BIBLE STUDY continued

B   AUTHORITY & POWER

2   In **Luke 10**, Jesus sent out 70 others, 2 by 2, and explained how they were to react to people and minister in various cities. (Some Bible translations state 72 were sent out)

- **Verses 8-12**   How were they to act in these cities and based on the reaction of the people they met, what did Jesus want them to say?

_____

_____

_____

_____

- **Verses 17** What did the 70 discover from their ministry trip?

_____

_____

3   Read **Matthew 10:16-20** and answer the questions in each section.

- **Verses 16-18**   What does Jesus tell them regarding the people they will face, and what they need to know?

_____

_____

_____

_____

- **Verses 19-20**   Who are they to rely on?

_____

_____

_____

4   Read **John 20:19-23**.   What did Jesus do to prepare and confirm that His disciples were ready to minister on His behalf as stated in **verses 21-23**?

_____

_____

_____

SUMMARIZE THE MAIN THOUGHTS FROM THE VERSES IN SECTION B

KINGDOM ENCOUNTER
MINISTRY – HEALING & DELIVERANCE – SESSION #11

IV   BIBLE STUDY continued

    C   SIN, REPENTANCE & FORGIVENESS – SALVATION

Ministering to people, just like Jesus and His disciples did, often involves addressing **SIN** issues; and leading them to **REPENTANCE**. Then followed by accepting and receiving **FORGIVENESS** by the ministry subject themselves, as well as forgiving others. This breaks the bondage of sin.

FIRST, we address **SIN.** The state of sinfulness can be described as **"an irresistible inner moral power which controls people."** Apostle Paul describes how sin affected him:

- ^{19}For the good that I will to do, I do not do; but the evil I will not to do, that I practice. ^{20} Now if I do what I will not to do, it is no longer I who do it, but sin that dwells in me.
  Romans 7:19-20

---

    1   Until we repent and are delivered from slavery to sin, we are eternally alienated from God. In these verses a few of the common areas of sin are mentioned.

        ▪ **Galatians 6:1** How would you minister to someone who is suffering under the weight of their sin?

_____

_____

_____

        ▪ **Matthew 23:28** What is the warning to believers?

_____

_____

        ▪ **Matthew 24:12** Explain how this is affecting our society.

_____

_____

        ▪ **Corinthians 6:14** How would this command keep us away from sin?

_____

REPENTANCE from any type of sin is required prior to receiving salvation. This means willingly turning from what we have done _that God considers to be sin_, and submitting to God as our Father, and Jesus Christ as our Lord and Savior.

---

    2   Give your understanding of the following verses regarding **REPENTANCE**.

        • **Psalm 32:5** Explain these steps to repentance.

_____

        • **2 Corinthians 7:10** What produces repentance?

_____

_____

KINGDOM ENCOUNTER
MINISTRY – HEALING & DELIVERANCE – SESSION #11

IV BIBLE STUDY continued

C SIN, REPENTANCE & FORGIVENESS – SALVATION

> **FORGIVENESS** of **SINS** following repentance is what leads to **SALVATION**. At the time of **SALVATION,** the believer receives full redemption and restoration by the blood of Jesus Christ.

3 **Explain the process as revealed in the following verses:**
- **Colossians 1:13-14** Explain the value of forgiveness.

_____

_____

- **1 John 1:9** What does confession do for us?

_____

_____

- **Jeremiah 31:34** What does the prophet Jeremiah explain that Jesus would do?

_____

_____

4 **Parable of the Prodigal Son** – Read **Luke 15:11-24**
- **Verses 18-24** Comment on how this is an illustration of God's love toward us and the pathway from **SIN** to **REPENTANTCE** to **FORGIVENESS** to **RESTORATION**

_____

_____

_____

> **FORGIVENSS TOWARD OTHERS** – in ministering to others you will find that repenting of holding offense against someone is required first. Then forgiveness takes place. Importantly, forgiveness does not mean they did nothing wrong, the believer is releasing their "hold" against that person and setting themselves free from the weight of "unforgiveness" (which is sin) they have carried.

5 **Matthew 6:14-15** What is the key point in the following verses?

_____

_____

_____

> **SALVATION** – Repentance, the forgiveness of sins, and salvation. When ministering to an unbeliever who comes to you for healing or deliverance, the Holy Spirit will show you where to start. Jesus sometimes healed them first, then addressed the issue of sin and repentance which leads to **SALVATION**.

6 Leading non-believers to **SALVATION** is addressed in the following verses:
- **Matthew 9:5-6** What is the connection between healing & forgiveness of sin?

_____

_____

IV BIBLE STUDY continued

C SIN, REPENTANCE & FORGIVENESS - SALVATION   continued

6   Leading non-believers to **SALVATION** is addressed in the following verses: ...continued

- **Ephesians 2:8-9**   How are we saved?

_____

_____

- **Acts 4:12**   In whose name do we pray to receive Salvation?

_____

_____

SUMMARIZE THE MAIN THOUGHTS FROM THE VERSES IN SECTION C

D   HEALING PHYSICAL AILMENTS

> All healing takes place by placing our Faith in the one who heals – Jesus Christ by the Power of His Holy Spirit. In ministry, our walk of faith, under the authority of Christ, allows the Holy Spirit to flow through us to heal the sick. It is never about us; and many times, the faith of the individual has nothing to do with their healing. Always be open to how **HOLY SPIRIT** chooses to heal someone to whom you are ministering. In this section, notice the part **FAITH** plays and the variety of ways people are healed.

1   In these verses the person who was healed was not present. Why do you think that happened? Explain your observations.
- **Matthew 8:13**

_____

_____

- **Matthew 15:28**

_____

_____

2   How were these people healed, and what was their sickness or physical issue?
- **Matthew 9:20-22**

_____

_____

_____

IV BIBLE STUDY continued
D HEALING PHYSICAL AILMENTS   continued

3   How were these people healed, and what was their sickness or physical issue? ...continued
   - **Matthew 9:23-26**

_____

_____

   - **Mark 7:32-35**

_____

_____

4   What does **Matthew 11:5** state is the ministry of Jesus?

_____

_____

5   Explain what **Mark 6:4-6** says about the ability to do miracles? How might this relate to our ministering to people under similar circumstances?

_____

_____

6   Within the church, how are people ministered to according to **James 5:14-16**? Notice how this relates to being part of a ministry team (often the elders of the church).

_____

_____

SUMMARIZE THE MAIN THOUGHTS FROM THE VERSES IN SECTION D

E DELIVERANCE – demons, strongholds, and inner healing

Jesus came to "set the captives free" from all human conditions that separate mankind from our Loving Father God. Which includes casting out evil spirits, breaking down strongholds we erect in our mind, and healing the heart and soul. We have received ALL AUTHORITY to accomplish this task in the Name of Jesus. Remember, it is not about us, but the Power of the Holy Spirit who does the work.

There are times that a person who is sick or physically impaired is also afflicted by evil spirits. The Holy Spirit will give you discernment to know if there is an evil spirit component with the disease or physical condition. The sickness is healed, and the demon is cast out. "Demonic Spirits" cannot be healed, only removed from the person by commanding them to leave. Followed by restoration, receiving the truth of the gospel, and being filled by the Peace of God and the Holy Spirit.

KINGDOM ENCOUNTER
MINISTRY – HEALING & DELIVERANCE – SESSION #11

IV **BIBLE STUDY continued**

   E   **DELIVERANCE – demons, strongholds and inner healing**   continued

      1 **RECOGNIZING THE ENEMY**

- Who is the enemy according to **Ephesians 6:12**?

_____

_____

- Where did the demonic forces come from as found in **Revelation 12:9**?
  Who are they?

_____

_____

      2 What is our objective in this spiritual war as found in **Acts 26:18?**

_____

_____

      3 Lessons from Jesus about casting out demons. Read **Matthew 12:22-29** and answer the questions in each group of verses:

- **Verses 22-24** This is an example of a physical condition together with demonic possession. What happened and what did the Pharisees say?

_____

_____

- **Verses 25-28** Notice that Jesus is describing two kingdoms. What are your thoughts?

_____

_____

> In **Matthew 12:29** Jesus explains how to accomplish deliverance from Satan/demonic forces: "Or how can one enter a strong man's house and plunder his goods, unless he first binds the strong man? And then he will plunder his house."
>
> The context of this verse is describing what believers must do to take back what belongs to the Kingdom of God. The term "Bind" was an idiomatic term used among the Jewish Rabbis (his audience) which meant to "prohibit" (forbid) from further activity. Jesus, who was speaking to Jewish Rabbis, was telling them that Satan (the Strongman) needed to be "prohibited" (bound) from controlling God's house. Once the spirit is "bound" (prohibited), it cannot exert any more control or pain over the afflicted person and then his "spiritual house" can be cleaned out. Give your comments on this situation. This will be a valuable area of discussion in your small group.

- After reading **Matthew 12:29** and the explanation regarding **DELIVERANCE,** give your comments on how this relates to ministering to someone afflicted by demons.

_____

_____

_____

IV BIBLE STUDY continued

E   DELIVERANCE – demons, strongholds and inner healing   continued

4   Much of **DELIVERANCE MINISTRY** involves setting people free from DEMONIC AFFLICTION (Possession and Oppression) this section will list some of the most common spirits. However, the Bible is more interested in teaching us to **RESIST THE ENEMY** than in helping us define him. In most cases, Jesus told demons to "come out" rather than asking their name. Jesus Christ has given us all power and authority over them! Reminder: *"He who is in you is greater than he who is in the world."* **1 John 4:4**

❖   This most useful verse in the Bible will strengthen your **FAITH** and **CONFIDENCE IN YOUR AUTHORITY**. Commit it to memory and use it to remind yourself and those that you minister to that it is the **POWER OF GOD**, the **HOLY SPIRIT**, that enables you to resist the devil and expel Him from your life.

■   **Write out: James 4:7 and commit it to memory.**

_____

_____

5   Evil Spirits are identified by the havoc they cause in our lives. All evil is to be "cast out." Rather than making an exhaustive list, here are a few of the ones found in scripture: INFIRMITY (Luke 13:11), BONDAGE/SLAVERY (Romans 8:15), FEAR/TIMIDITY (2 Timothy 1:7), HEAVINESS (Isaiah 61:3), DIVINATION/WITCHCRAFT (Acts 16:16).   *There are three types of demonic spirits listed below we feel should be mentioned in more detail. Explain your findings.*

●   **Matthew 12:43-45   #1**   What does this spirit do and why is it particularly dangerous in the life of an individual?

_____

_____

_____

_____

●   **Revelation 2:20   #2   Spirit of Jezebel** (This spirit operates by lying, gossip and deception. Ref: **1 Kings**; she was the wife of King Ahab. She did not repent). Like all demonic spirits, she must be cast out of the individual. Have you seen this spirit active in any church or ministry you have been a part of? Describe.

_____

_____

_____

_____

_____

IV   BIBLE STUDY continued
E   DELIVERANCE – demons, strongholds and inner healing   continued

5   There are three types of spirits listed below we feel should be mentioned in more detail. Explain your findings.   Continued

---

#3 FAMILIAR SPIRITS. In **1 Samuel 28:3** we read: "And Saul had put away those that had familiar spirits, and the wizards, out of the land." **FAMILIAR SPIRITS** afflict people from generation to generation. They try to entice people with secrets about themselves, their family, or others. They often bring with them a **LYING SPIRIT. The FAMILIAR SPIRIT**, knowing an individual's family history, will entice a person to consult with demonic and unclean spirits through divination and soothsaying. (Ouija Boards, Tarot Cards, Palm Readers, Channeling, Rebirthing, and other new age practices – all work with familiar spirits).

- You may see the effects of **FAMILIAR SPIRITS** in individuals seeking deliverance, and they are dealt with the same as others – **CAST THEM OUT! Your thoughts?**

_____

_____

6   Another important aspect of the **DELIVERANCE MINISTRY** involves **INNER HEALING.**

Addressing issues of the heart and soul (Our mind, will and emotions) and dealing with what has entered our mind, either accidentally due to trauma or other circumstances beyond our control, or consciously through acceptance of false teaching, wrong ideas, or sin. The result is sadness, fear, depression, anxiety, even physical ailments. This area of **DELIVERANCE** involves breaking strongholds – wrong patterns of thought, renouncing agreements made with false ideas, ceasing sinful activities – then accepting and focusing on the truth found in the Word of God. The result is a wonderful peace residing in the heart and mind.

In the following verses observe how one's strongholds are broken:

- **2 Corinthians 10:3-5** The key point is found in **verse 5** – explain a practical application.

_____

_____

- **Romans 12:2** How would a practical application of this verse help set one free from strongholds in the mind?

_____

_____

- **1 Peter 5:6-7** What is our act of humility, and what is the result?

_____

_____

_____

KINGDOM ENCOUNTER
MINISTRY – HEALING & DELIVERANCE – SESSION #11

IV **BIBLE STUDY** continued

    E   **DELIVERANCE – demons, strongholds and inner healing**   **continued**

        6   Regarding **INNER HEALING**......Observe from these verses how one's strongholds are broken. ...continued

            • **Philippians 4:7** Once set free, what guards/protects your heart and mind?

_____

_____

_____

            • **Colossians 3:2-3** Regarding inner healing, which is a "Soul"- mind/will/emotions) issue – how does one stay free?

_____

_____

SUMMARIZE THE MAIN THOUGHTS FROM THE VERSES IN SECTION E

    F   **FREEDOM - HEALED & DELIVERED**

The purpose of all **MINISTRY** is to point God's children to the **KINGDOM OF GOD**, to living a Kingdom Lifestyle in this world and having faith in God that it will continue in eternity. Ministry in Jesus Christ is helping people stay **FREE – HEALED & DELIVERED**!

        1   These verses illustrate how to accept the truth of our healing and deliverance by faith, and live in **FREEDOM** in the Lord Jesus Christ based on the **WORD OF GOD**:

            • **Psalm 91:9-10** This Psalm speaks of the "secret place" available to all believers.   In these verses, what are the benefits to the believer?

_____

_____

            • **Proverbs 3:5-6** How does this command keep you free?

_____

_____

            • **Isaiah 53:4-5** What does the last line in **verse five** say about healing?

_____

_____

KINGDOM ENCOUNTER
MINISTRY – HEALING & DELIVERANCE – SESSION #11

IV **BIBLE STUDY continued**

    F   **FREEDOM – HEALED & DELIVERED**   continued

        1 These verses illustrate how to accept the truth of our healing and deliverance by faith, and live in FREEDOM in the Lord Jesus Christ based on the WORD OF GOD: ...continued

            • **Matthew 26:41**   What keeps us from falling into temptation?

_____

_____

            • **John 8:35-36**   How does this verse confirm our identity?

_____

_____

_____

        2 In **John 5:14** and **John 8:11** what was the command Jesus gave to those He healed/delivered?

_____

_____

_____

        3 The following verses give practical advice for living in **FREEDOM**:

            • **Philippians 4:8**   How would the items listed in this verse help one stay **FREE**?

_____

_____

            • **Galatians 5:1**   How is our liberty at stake?

_____

_____

            • **Galatians 5:22-23** How would you use the fruit of the Spirit to live a **KINGDOM LIFESTYLE**?

_____

_____

SUMMARIZE THE MAIN THOUGHTS FROM THE VERSES IN SECTION F

KINGDOM ENCOUNTER
MINISTRY – HEALING & DELIVERANCE – SESSION #11

V SUMMARY & APPLICATION

SUMMARY - Write out the verse that is most meaningful to you from each section in this study.

A EMPOWERED FOR MINISTRY
B AUTHORITY & POWER
C SIN, REPENTANCE & FORGIVENESS - SALVATION
D HEALING PHYSICAL AILMENTS
E DELIVERANCE – DEMONS, STRONGHOLDS, AND INNER HEALING
F FREEDOM – HEALED & DELIVERED

APPLICATION - think about these questions, write your thoughts if you wish to do so, or save them for class discussion.

1   What was your most important discovery about **MINISTRY – HEALING & DELIVERANCE**?

_____

_____

_____

2   What area of ministering in **HEALING & DELIVERANCE** are you currently applying in your life?

_____

_____

_____

3   What helps you stay FREE?

_____

_____

_____

_____

_____

NOTES

KINGDOM ENCOUNTER

KINGDOM WEALTH
SESSION #12

KINGDOM WEALTH can be described as the benefits we receive
as Kings and Priests in His Kingdom on earth and in eternity.
The KINGDOM LIFESTYLE we are privileged to enjoy with our family,
in ministry, and in the marketplace reflects who we are as children of God.

This session will deepen your understanding that it is God who gives you
"power to get wealth" and that He "delights in the prosperity of His people."
The primary motivational force is God's love for us and that through love
we would manage KINGDOM WEALTH to serve one another.

KINGDOM ENCOUNTER
Our Group Prayer Sheet

MEMBERS:

	Name	Email	Cell Phone
1			
2			
3			
4			

Praises & Prayer Requests

"As for me, far be it from me that I should sin against the Lord by failing to pray for you." 1 Samuel 12:23

Date	Praises/Prayer Requests	Date	Answers

KINGDOM ENCOUNTER
KINGDOM WEALTH – SESSION #12

I   INTRODUCTION:

KINGDOM WEALTH can be described as the benefits we receive as Kings and Priests in His Kingdom on earth and in eternity. The **KINGDOM LIFESTYLE** we are privileged to enjoy with our family, in ministry, and in the marketplace reflects who we are as children of God, heirs to His promises. In the beginning we were given authority to take dominion, fill the earth and subdue it. Access to all the wealth of the **KINGDOM OF GOD** is our inheritance. Christ has *"redeemed us to God by (His blood) out of every tribe and tongue and people and nation and have made us kings and priests to our God; and we shall reign on the earth."* **Revelation 5:9-10 (NKJV)**

This session will deepen your understanding that it is God who gives you "power to get wealth" and that He "delights in the prosperity of His people." The primary motivational force is God's love for us and that through love we would manage **KINGDOM WEALTH** to serve one another. You will witness through this session that His blessing is on those who wisely manage the wealth and possessions He has given us. We bring him glory and honor when we use our wealth to multiply His Kingdom!

II   GOD SPEAKS TO YOU THROUGH HIS WORD: write out the memory verse.

A   MEMORY VERSE: **Psalm 112:1-3**

B   Analysis Questions

1   What is promised to a man who fears the Lord?

_____

_____

_____

_____

2   Who receives the blessings of the Lord when a man is righteous?

_____

_____

_____

_____

3   What will be the condition of his house?

_____

_____

_____

_____

_____

KINGDOM ENCOUNTER
KINGDOM WEALTH – SESSION #12

III DEFINE: KINGDOM WEALTH (Using Biblical resources)

_____

_____

_____

IV BIBLE STUDE

A ESTABLISHING KINGDOM WEALTH

1 In the beginning God created His **KINGDOM ON EARTH** as a reflection of His **KINGDOM IN HEAVEN**, one of beauty, wealth, and abundance. He established the earthly kingdom through two families. In the following verses what was their mandate?

- **Genesis 1:28**

_____

- **Genesis 9:1**

_____

2 What was God's vision for His Kingdom when He chose Abram as reflected in

- **Genesis 12:1-3**?

_____

3 In the following verses notice how and why Abram became wealthy in land and possessions:

- **Genesis 12:7** What was Abram's response to the Lord?

_____

- **Genesis 13:1-3** Why was Abram blessed?

_____

- **Genesis 13:14-15** Why do you suppose God had not shown Abram before this moment the extent of what he planned to give him?

_____

- **Genesis 14:18-20** What was God confirming to Abram? What did Abram do in response?

_____

KINGDOM ENCOUNTER
KINGDOM WEALTH – SESSION #12

IV **BIBLE STUDY continued**

   A **ESTABLISHING KINGDOM WEALTH**   **continued**

     4   When Abram discussed with God the fact that he had no heir to all the wealth God had given him, what did God do? Read **Genesis 15:4-7**.

_____

_____

     5   In **Genesis 17:2-8** what was the significance of the "name change" and what was the extent of the blessings of wealth he was to pass to his generations?

_____

_____

     6   Reflecting on how God blessed Abraham so that he prospered in every way, and Abraham believed and was accounted righteous, how does that become our **KINGDOM** mandate?

        • **Galatians 3:13-14**

_____

_____

SUMMARIZE THE MAIN THOUGHTS FROM THE VERSES IN SECTION A

   B **BLESSED TO BE A BLESSING**

     As God prospered Abraham, we explore in this section the lives of wealthy individuals highlighted throughout scripture. Notice how they lived and treated others around them. In the Kingdom of God, wealth that endures through generations occurs when one is blessed to be a blessing. ***"Now be pleased to bless the house of your servant, that it may continue forever in your sight; for you, Sovereign LORD, have spoken, and with your blessing the house of your servant will be blessed forever."*** **2 Samuel 7:29**

     1   Job was an extremely wealthy man; and he was generous toward his family and friends, and He loved God. Yet God allowed Satan to test Job and destroy his family and take away his possessions. Read Job 1 for the details. Refer to the following verses and answer the questions.

        • **Job's wealth – verse 1:3**   What was the extent of Job's wealth?

_____

_____

IV BIBLE STUDY continued

B BLESSED TO BE A BLESSING   continued

1 Job was an extremely wealthy man...... continued

- Job's response to loss – **verses 1:20-22**   When Job had everything in life taken from him, how did he respond?   How might this help you respond differently when/if you are faced with terrible circumstances?

_____

_____

_____

- Job's wealth and position are restored by God – **verses 42:10**   Explain what God saw in Job that he restored and blessed him.   What is the practical application for your own life?

_____

_____

_____

2 **Jabez**   Read **1 Chronicles 4:9-10** and comment on why he wanted God to change the circumstances in his life.   How might you use his prayer in your own life?

_____

_____

_____

3 **Boaz**, a wealthy landowner, became the husband of Ruth and together are the great-great-grandparents of King David. In this example learn how blessings flow through the generations.   Notice from the life of Boaz how he used his wealth, his position, and the importance of integrity in treating employees, family, and friends. The book of Ruth is an excellent model of the application of **KINGDOM WEALTH** principles.

- **Ruth 2:1-2**   Naomi, her husband (Elimelech) and both sons had died. She and her daughter-in-law returned to the city of her husband's family. Why did Ruth ask to work in the field of Boaz?

_____

_____

_____

- **Ruth 2:4**   What is the level of respect Boaz has with the field workers?

_____

_____

_____

KINGDOM ENCOUNTER
KINGDOM WEALTH – SESSION #12

IV BIBLE STUDY continued

   B BLESSED TO BE A BLESSING   continued

      2 The book of Ruth is an excellent model of the application of **KINGDOM WEALTH** principles. ...Continued

- **Ruth 2:8-9** What does Boaz do for Ruth?   How does he watch out for her safety.

_____

_____

_____

- **Ruth 3:9-11** What can you observe here about appropriate relationships?   And the integrity and honor Boaz shows toward Ruth.

_____

_____

_____

- **Ruth 4:10-11** Describe what you observe is the value of inheritance, the blessings for generations, and comment on why Boaz is held in such high esteem.

_____

_____

_____

      3 **David – King of Israel**   Read these verses from the life of King David and make your observations as the Holy Spirit reveals practical application for your own life.

- **Acts 13:22**   David became a wealthy man, what is the simple explanation?

_____

_____

- **1 Chronicles 28**   These verses illustrate how God directed David to transfer his wealth and kingdom to the one He chose from David's sons.
    - ➢ **Verses 2-3**   Why didn't God allow David to use his wealth to build a temple for Him?

_____

_____

- ➢ **Verses 9-10**   What was the fatherly advice David gave to Solomon?

_____

_____

IV BIBLE STUDY continued

B BLESSED TO BE A BLESSING   continued

4   David – King of Israel   …continued

- **1 Chronicles 28**   These verses illustrate how God directed David to transfer his wealth and kingdom to the one He chose from David's sons.   **…continued**
    - ➤ **Verses 11-18** Physical transfer of David's wealth to Solomon. In **Verse 12a** How did David know what to give to Solomon?   How might God's directive to David inform our decisions regarding our own legacy planning for our children and grandchildren?

_____

_____

    - ➤ **Verse 19**   How did the Lord make David aware of His plan? What is the practical application of how God reveals His plans for you?

_____

_____

5   Solomon – Son of David

- **2 Chronicles 1:11-12**   Why did he become the richest man that has ever lived?

_____

_____

6   Joseph from Arimathea

- **Matthew 27:57-60**   How did he use his wealth at this important time in history?

_____

_____

7   Zacchaeus

- **Luke 19:1-10**   What compelled Zacchaeus to transform his life from being selfish to generous?

_____

_____

_____

SUMMARIZE THE MAIN THOUGHTS FROM THE VERSES IN SECTION B

IV   BIBLE STUDY continued
C   GOD'S SYSTEM OF WEALTH

The Bible has more to say on money and financial management than any other topic. Bad theology says that "money is the root of all evil." Like so many popular beliefs, that statement is taken out of context. It is **THE LOVE OF MONEY:** "For the love of money is a root of all kinds of evil, for which some have strayed from the faith in their greediness and pierced themselves through with many sorrows." **1 Timothy 6:10**. The facts, as we have seen, are that wealth appropriately managed is a blessing for everyone and funds the Kingdom of God on earth through all generations. Poverty blesses no one.

In this section we focus on God's principles for creating and managing money and resources.

Ecclesiastes 10:18-19   What is Solomon's observation about lack of diligence and having sufficient provision? Comment on what he says about money.

_____

_____

1   GOD IS YOUR SOURCE.
- **Malachi 3:10**   What is God's promise regarding our ability to be financially blessed?

_____

_____

- **Luke 6:38**   What is required first, before we can expect to receive?

_____

_____

- **Philippians 4:19**   Are there any limits to how your needs are met? Explain your thoughts.

_____

_____

- **2 Thessalonians 3:10**   What is the value of work? How is that applicable to today's society?

_____

_____

- **Psalm 90:17**   Who establishes the work of our hands?

_____

_____

- **Deuteronomy 8:18**   What does it mean to "remember the Lord your God?" Why is that important?

_____

_____

_____

KINGDOM ENCOUNTER
KINGDOM WEALTH – SESSION #12

IV **BIBLE STUDY continued**

  C   **GOD'S SYSTEMS OF WEALTH**   continued

    2   **BUSINESS CREATES WEALTH**. Whether self-employed or working for another - this is God's system to create wealth. Business is the exchange of goods or services for profit or gain.

- **Luke 19:13** What did the employer ask his servants to do while he was away; how should they have responded?

_____

_____

- **Proverbs 13:22** From your experience what is a practical application of this verse?

_____

_____

- **Luke 16:12** What does this say about how we treat another person's business? How does it affect what we do in a restaurant, renting a car or hotel room, how we treat other people who provide services?

_____

_____

    3   **ALL BUSINESS REQUIRES WORK.**

- **Proverbs 14:23** What is the value of work?

_____

_____

- **Proverbs 30:25** Comment on diligence and teamwork in proper season

_____

_____

    4   **BUSINESS IS A PROVING GROUND.** Look at **Psalm 1:1-3** as a business plan – how do you set yourself up for success? Comment on your findings.

- **Verse 1** Who to listen to, stay away from, and where to build a business.

_____

_____

- **Verse 2** Who is your primary business partner?

_____

_____

- **Verse 3** Positioning oneself to be in the "flow", the right timing, and the expectation of success.

_____

_____

_____

KINGDOM ENCOUNTER
KINGDOM WEALTH – SESSION #12

IV BIBLE STUDY continued
   C GOD'S SYSTEM OF WEALTH   continued
   5 THE TRANSFER OF WEALTH IS WORK RELATED
   - **Proverbs 13:22b NIV** Does this mean that we have a right to what belongs to another if we do nothing? Your thoughts?

   _____
   _____
   _____

   - **2 Kings 4:1-7**   Read the story of the widow who only had "a small jar of olive oil." What did she have to do to realize a supernatural wealth transfer?   What is a practical application, or a miracle, that maybe you have experienced when faced with insufficient provision?

   _____
   _____
   _____

   6 RECLAIMING OUR TERRITORY. God gave us authority and commanded mankind to subdue and take dominion – to establish His **KINGDOM** on earth. Many believers have become complacent. How do we turn this around and take back what belongs to God's children?
   - **Deuteronomy 28:13**   How does positioning become important?

   _____
   _____
   _____

   - **Deuteronomy 7:9** What is required for generational blessings?

   _____
   _____
   _____

   - **Isaiah 58:1**   In what ways does this relate to our society and what we may be called to do?

   _____
   _____
   _____

SUMMARIZE THE MAIN THOUGHTS FROM THE VERSES IN SECTION C

KINGDOM ENCOUNTER
KINGDOM WEALTH – SESSION #12

IV BIBLE STUDY continued
D GENERATIONAL WEALTH

The Bible is generational and legacy minded. Exhaustive genealogies abound throughout scripture illustrating God's value on fulfilling His commandment to multiply. What does that have to do with wealth? The legacy of family businesses pass to the next generation. We are reminded of the importance of providing an inheritance for our grandchildren. In financial planning terms we might call this "Legacy Planning." In this section we review what the Bible says about this topic for His faithful followers.

Remember that in Christ there is neither Jew nor Gentile, we are all one. We *"...were grafted in among them, and with them became a partaker of the root and fatness of the olive tree (Israel)."* **Romans 11:17**

Generational wealth includes being established as kings (authority), and priests in our family, in ministry and the marketplace. Describe your findings in the following verses:

- **Psalm 89:4** This was a promise to King David; but prophecy can flow by the Holy Spirit to other believers for their benefit. Ask **HOLY SPIRIT** what this verse might mean for your future. Give your comments.

_____

- **Proverbs 13:22a** What does this say about the value of financial management?

_____

_____

- **Numbers 18:21** What does God say about the level of provision due those who work in ministry?

_____

_____

- **Numbers 36:9** What does God say about one's inheritance staying within the family? Why do you think that would be important?

_____

_____

- **Deuteronomy 19:14** Property boundaries were established as a principle that has carried over into our society and real estate transactions today. Why do you think that is important?

_____

_____

_____

KINGDOM ENCOUNTER
KINGDOM WEALTH – SESSION #12

IV BIBLE STUDY continued

D GENERATIONAL WEALTH   continued

Generational wealth includes being established as kings (authority), and priests in our family, in ministry and the marketplace. Describe your findings in the following verses: ...continued

- **I Chronicles 28:8**   Before possessing land and considering our inheritance, what comes first; and why?

_____

_____

- **Ezra 9:12**   What can we learn here that should be considered when making life choices – marriage, establishing business, and future generations?

_____

_____

- **Proverbs 19:14**   Why is it important that a wife come from the Lord? Especially coupled with watching over an inheritance of houses and riches.

_____

_____

- **Proverbs 20:21**   Why is this inheritance not blessed?

_____

_____

- **Ecclesiastes 7:11**   Give your thoughts on why WISDOM is important for managing wealth.

_____

_____

- **Ezekiel 46:18**   What does God command Rulers/Kings/Princes who oversee their subjects?

_____

_____

- **Hebrews 11:8** Describe the obedience of Abraham and how this applies to you when you consider establishing your future legacy.

_____

_____

SUMMARIZE THE MAIN THOUGHTS FROM THE VERSES IN SECTION D

KINGDOM ENCOUNTER
KINGDOM WEALTH – SESSION #12

V SUMMARY & APPLICATION

SUMMARY - Write out the verse that is most meaningful to you from each section in this study.

A ESTABLISHING KINGDOM WEALTH

B BLESSED TO BE A BLESSING

C GOD'S SYSTEM OF WEALTH

D GENERATIONAL WEALTH

APPLICATION - think about these questions, write your thoughts if you wish to do so, or save them for class discussion.

1 Are there any thoughts about establishing wealth that you found helpful?

2 What are some ways that you find to bless others and then see blessings increase in your own life?

3 Did you discover anything new about generational wealth or legacy planning?

NOTES

NOTES

NOTES

BIBLIOGRAPHY

The Kingdom Encounter is entirely based on the Word of God by using various Bible translations to clarify points and bring understanding.

1. **New Spirit-Filled Life Bible (NKJV),** Executive Editor Jack W Hayford, 2002 by Thomas Nelson, Inc.   This is the primary source Bible for scriptural references except where indicated in the book.

2. **Biblegateway.com** (Online app for desktop and mobile) (All quotations from other Bible translations were taken off this site)

ABOUT THE AUTHORS

September 29, 1986, Michael & Michele Kole accepted Jesus Christ as their Lord and Savior. After 4 years of marriage, 2 small children, financial loss, marriage in shambles, and separation – we accepted the Lord when Ps John Maxwell, Skyline Wesleyan Church, Lemon Grove, CA, gave the altar call. What followed soon after was one-on-one discipleship with a wonderful older couple who poured into our lives individually for a year. We credit their faithfulness with grounding us in the Bible and laying the foundation that would last and is the reason we value discipleship in the Word of God – His manual for how to do life.

Their backgrounds are very different. Michael was born in Yugoslavia, of Serbian parents, during WW2. His father was a shepherd, and he was born in a "manger". (True story!). The house where they lived was damaged during the war, and they lived in what was left, in the basement with the animals. His father fought against the Communists, and he was shot and captured, but escaped to get the family out of the country when Michael was 6 months old. They walked out on foot in the winter, across the border to Italy. Michael, his parents and 2 brothers, lived in refugee camps in Italy and Germany before immigrating to the United States when he was 6 years old. He lived in Chicago where his mom and dad worked in factories, then owned a bar and restaurant and his father became a plumber. Michael graduated from the University of Illinois at Chicago, served stateside in the Army during Viet Nam, then became a successful real estate broker until moving to San Diego in 1978. He was raised in the Serbian Orthodox Church.

Michele was born in San Diego, California, to parents who were born in Iowa and Indiana. Her mom was a pastor's daughter, her dad was Catholic. Her mom stayed at home to take care of her and her 2 sisters, while her dad worked for the Navy in civil service. Michele graduated from San Diego State University, worked in property management, then became a real estate broker and later a mortgage broker. Michele attended the Presbyterian church until college when her mom switched to the Methodist church.

ABOUT THE AUTHORS
Page 2

In 1978 Michael and Michele happened to be taking disco dancing lessons at a local restaurant and bar. They had one date but ran into each other occasionally in various real estate and networking groups. One night in February of 1981, bells and whistles went off at another local dance place and that was it. They married on November 7, 1982. One year later their son, Jason, was born. From the outside all looked wonderful! But it wasn't. They both had been attracted to New Age teaching and practices – were in fact married in a Church of Religious Science. Got involved in areas such as "teachings of the Inner Christ" (demonic), rebirthing, body work modalities, calling up spirits, table tipping, EST, and anything New Age they could find. All of which left them empty, confused, oppressed, and depressed. Their business went under, they lost their home, their cars, they had just had a baby girl; and their son was only 2-1/2. Michele moved back home to live with her parents, Michael left for Chicago to restart their business with his family.

BUT GOD… A faithful friend of Michael and Michele prayed for them. Michael returned from Chicago to get back with Michele. Her parents and family were not on board and forbid him from staying at their home. It was decided that they would attend church together at their friend's invitation. It was at Skyline Wesleyan Church, where they accepted the Lord, were discipled and God put their marriage back together after the year of discipleship was completed. The next year Michele gave birth to their son, Jeremy. Their family was complete.

God has been the center of their lives since 1986. Through many challenging times they have thrived and grown stronger. Each church and ministry they have joined has helped them build a strong foundation in the Word of God and understanding the value of discipleship, and especially in developing home groups and multiplying them. In 1993 they were led to write a discipleship program called the "SPIRIT LED LIFE" which is still available via the internet and in some churches. Seasons of ministry have brought them through many denominational teachings and eventually into evangelistic and charismatic ministries. They were baptized in the Holy Spirit around 2000 (each at different times as Michele was a bit resistant). They were ordained in 2005 by Ps George Runyan with Ps Alan Higgins at the Life Church in San Diego. Then spent several years in the G12 ministry learning and teaching cell group leadership, having Encounter Weekends, growing in ministry in aspects of healing and deliverance. Since 2012 they have been a part of Awaken Church San Diego, a youth-oriented spirit filled ministry, where they oversee the PRIME Ministry (for age 50+), are Connect Group Coaches, and are on the ministry and pastoral care teams. In the past few years, the Holy Spirit has spoken to them about a new discipleship series focused on the KINGDOM OF GOD. They began preparing diligently for about 4 years, not knowing when this would come together. Holy Spirit said NOW in December 2022! In January 2023 the first session of the KINGDOM ENCOUNTER DISCIPLESHIP was launched.

Having a KINGDOM MINDSET, Michael and Michele are in business together, with over 4 decades each in real estate and financial services. Their company is called the Financial Strategies Team (FST) and oversees teams of professionals who provide services for FST. The real estate team includes sales, 1031 exchanges and structured sales to mitigate capital gains taxes. The lending team provides reverse mortgages. The financial planning division includes retirement planning, insurance and estate planning which includes wills and trusts to avoid probate. The FINANCIAL STRATEGIES TEAM synergistically maximizes benefits to their clients.

ABOUT THE AUTHORS
Page 3

Michael and Michele just celebrated 40 years of marriage, love spending time with their two sons and one daughter with their amazing spouses, and especially enjoy their 10 grandchildren.

For more information contact:
Michael Kole @ 858-848-4274, or Michele Kole @ 858-344-5998
Email: michaelkole1@gmail.com, michelekole@gmail.com
We are delighted to answer questions and help you begin the discipleship journey with your church or small group of disciples.

Made in the USA
Columbia, SC
25 July 2023

20806929R10115